# Caricature Carvers of America

•

# *Thinking Inside the Roughout*

SCHIFFER PUBLISHING
4880 Lower Valley Road • Atglen, PA 19310

Designed by Sandy Smith
Type set in Myriad Pro/Adobe Caslon Pro/Elephant

ISBN: 978-0-7643-5782-4
Printed in China

**CCA Book Committee:** Sandy Smith, Editor; Randy Landen and Bob Travis, Associate Editors.

**Studio photographs:** Jack A and Carole Williams; Step-by-Step photographs by Randy Landen.

Published by Schiffer Publishing, Ltd.
4880 Lower Valley Road
Atglen, PA 19310
Phone: (610) 593-1777; Fax: (610) 593-2002
E-mail: Info@schifferbooks.com

For our complete selection of fine books on this and related subjects, please visit our website at **www.schifferbooks.com.** You may also write for a free catalog.

This book may be purchased from the publisher. Please try your bookstore first.

We are always looking for people to write books on new and related subjects. If you have an idea for a book, please contact us at proposals@schifferbooks.com

Schiffer Publishing's titles are available at special discounts for bulk purchases for sales promotions or premiums. Special editions, including personalized covers, corporate imprints, and excerpts can be created in large quantities for special needs. For more information, contact the publisher.

This book is dedicated
to the memory of eight CCA members
who contributed greatly
to promoting
the art of caricature carving:

Claude Bolton

Tom Brown

Dave Dunham

Tex Haase

Will Hayden

Steve Prescott

Dave Rasmussen

Joe Wannamaker

# CONTENTS

# Who Are the Caricature Carvers of America?

**Active Members 2019**

David Boone
Steve Brown
Mitch Cartledge
Ron Dowdy
PJ Driscoll
Gary Falin
Dale Green
Chris Hammack
Bruce Henn
Jim Hiser
Randy Landen
Wayne Laramore
Pete LeClair
Ryan Olsen
Floyd Rhadigan
Joe Schumacher
Sandy Smith
Dave Stetson
Dennis Thornton
Bob Travis
Rich Wetherbee
Jack A Williams
Tom Wolfe
Joe You

**Emeritus Members**

Gary Batte
Phil Bishop
Vicki Bishop
Harold Enlow
Gene Fuller
Desiree Hajny
Eldon Humphreys
Marv Kaisersatt
Don Mertz
Keith Morrill
Peter Ortel
Vic Otto
Jack Price
Doug Raine
Harley Refsal
David Sabol
Harley Schmitgen
Gerald Sears
Cleve Taylor

**Deceased Members**

Claude Bolton
Tom Brown
Dave Dunham
Tex Haase
Will Hayden
Steve Prescott
Dave Rasmussen
Joe Wannamaker

## History of the Caricature Carvers of America

The publication of this book (our eighth) is a continuation of the mission of the CCA, originally envisioned by our founding members in 1990. Established as a nonprofit educational corporation, the CCA is dedicated to the following principles:

1. Promote and elevate the appreciation of the art of caricature woodcarving within the woodcarving community and the public.
2. Provide an environment that will encourage growth in skill, creativity, and excellence among its members and all carvers.

Over our 29-year history, the CCA has worked diligently to advance the art of woodcarving, and to encourage caricature carvers from around the world. To that end, the CCA has promoted caricature carving through exhibitions, seminars, our National Caricature Carving Competition, and the publication of eight distinctive books that focus on the art of caricature carving. Our roster of members, past and present, includes a diverse group of carvers, authors, and instructors who have inspired a generation of woodcarvers, including each of us.

Over the past three decades, the art of caricature carving has evolved rapidly, increasing in prominence and creativity. We are pleased to have been a part, however small, of that evolution.

Here is a short list of our major projects to date:

1991: Inaugural CCA exhibit opens at the National Museum of Woodcarving in Custer, South Dakota.
1995: Publication of our first book, *Carving the Full Moon Saloon*
1997: *Carving the Caricature Carvers of America Circus* is released
2000: The *CCA Signature Collection* is distributed on CD
2002: Launch of CCA's National Caricature Carving Competition
2007: *Caricature Carvers Showcase* is released
2009: *Carving an 1880s Western Train* is published
2010: Featured Exhibit at Silver Dollar City's 50th Anniversary Celebration
2011: Our fifth book, *Caricatures in Motion*, is published
2012: The CCA Train is the featured exhibit at the California Railroad Museum in Sacramento
2013: Publication of *Carving a 1930s Street Scene*
2015: Release of *Concepts to Caricatures: Celebrating 25 Years of Caricature Carving*
2019: Publication of *Thinking Inside the Roughout*

The success of any organization is directly attributable to the support it receives from outside the group. We have been fortunate to have the extraordinary backing of the carving community, our publishers, our competition partners at the Eastern Woodland Carvers Club, Inc., and the host of carving clubs and carving organizations throughout the US and Canada who work every day to support woodcarving as an art form.

# Overview

*O*ne question that we are frequently asked is "How do you folks come up with ideas for your books?" To answer, our projects have all evolved in one of two ways. One or more members may present an idea during our annual meeting and, following some discussion, it may be accepted or rejected. Examples of projects that evolved from this approach include *Caricature Carvers Showcase*, *Caricatures in Motion*, and *Concepts to Caricatures*. Alternatively, those suggesting a topic may present a mockup (cardboard, or full-scale carving) to underscore their idea. Examples of this approach include *Carving the Full Moon Saloon*, *Carving the CCA Circus*, *Carving an 1880s Western Train*, and *Carving a 1930s Street Scene*.

In all of our projects, our members work in the privacy of their studios. Most of us have no idea what others are carving. We purposely keep the rules simple. The scale is usually set at one inch to the foot, and carvings must be suitable for family entertainment. Other than that, there are no rules. We know from experience that all will be fine when we get together for the next meeting. That happened with our first project, the *Full Moon Saloon*, and has continued to work with successive projects.

The agenda for our 2016 annual meeting contained an item titled "Suggestions for our next book project." That day, four potential projects were presented. After discussing each proposal, the members voted unanimously to accept the "Universal Roughout Project." The following day we designed a generic roughout, making sure to leave excess wood in strategic places to provide maximum flexibility in designing the carving.

So, what happened this time? With this group, one never knows what to expect. Some made use of the excess wood to add all sorts of things to their carving. Others used the excess wood to exaggerate body proportions, while some just carved away the excess wood and did their own thing. One member even cut out the lower midsection of the roughout, glued the rest back together, and carved a short caricature. Interestingly enough, we have four pirates, three cooks, and two cross-dressers.

Here is our challenge to you. There are many roughouts available to carvers, virtually all of which have been designed for a specific purpose. The next time you purchase an extra roughout, use your creativity to see what else you might carve. Think inside the roughout, as you are limited by the wood available in the roughout. Try some of our examples to enhance your ability to see other things in a blank. Then branch out on your own, be creative, and have fun.

The roughout used in this book may be purchased on our website: www.cca-carvers.org

# Randy Landen

## "The Not-So-Thin Blue Line"

Randy Landen lives in Derby, Kansas, just south of Wichita. Randy began carving in 1990, at the Woodcarving Rendezvous in Branson, Missouri. His carvings are heavily influenced by the situations he encountered during his 33 years on the Wichita Police Department. Randy retired from policing in 2013, and is currently the Director, Executive Protection at Koch Industries in Wichita.

His love for carving began in 1977, when he and his wife, Carol, bought their first woodcarving at Silver Dollar City in Branson. Although they enjoy a wide range of carving styles, caricatures dominate their woodcarving collection. Randy has given carving and painting seminars across the US and served as judge at a variety of woodcarving shows throughout the country, including the International Woodcarvers Congress in Maquoketa, Iowa.

Randy enjoys repairing damaged carvings and sells a diverse variety of original carvings on the secondary market through his website. Please go to www.landenwoodcarving.com and click on "Carvings for Sale."

Contact info:
Randy Landen
PO Box 565 • Derby, KS 67037
rlanden@prodigy.net

Visit Randy's website: www.landenwoodcarving.com

# Step-by-Step Instructions

I was a police officer for 33 years. Throughout my career, there seemed to be a socially imposed relationship between cops and donuts. That allegory, real or imagined, served as the inspiration for this carving.

What makes this book project unique is the diversity of carvings that began life as the same roughout.

In the end, the carvings could not be more different. Each carver has their own unique approach to a project . . . here's mine.

# Step-by-Step with Randy Landen, *continued*

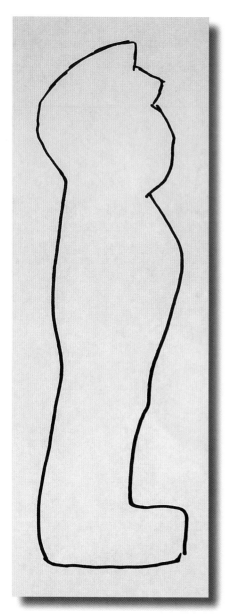

## ROUGHOUT

Unlike my fellow carvers Phil Bishop and Harold Enlow, I cannot draw a finished design on paper and translate that to wood. Instead, I know in my mind what I want to carve, and draw a rough outline directly onto the wood. I start by developing a raw shape in wood, or in this case, roughing out the roughout.

The first step is to find the centerline for the front of the carving, which for this piece is slightly to the left. The second step is to find the centerline for the side view. I primarily use three tools to rough out a carving: a carving knife, a wide #5 gouge, and a large "U" gouge.

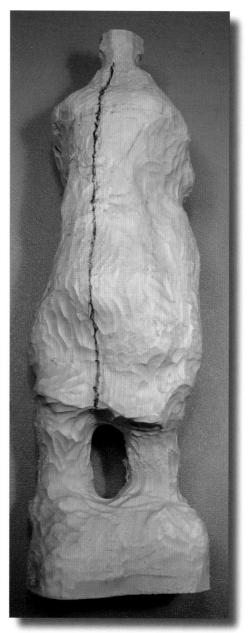

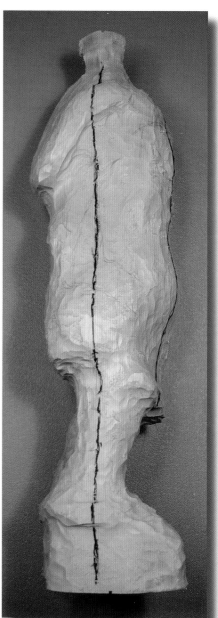

I draw general shapes for the head and arms on the wood and start to rough out the piece. Make a mental list of the areas where extra wood is needed, such as the tie, pockets, epaulets, bullets, and handcuff pouch. Locate them on the roughout in pencil or marker, use a V-tool to outline them on the carving, and start to refine the design.

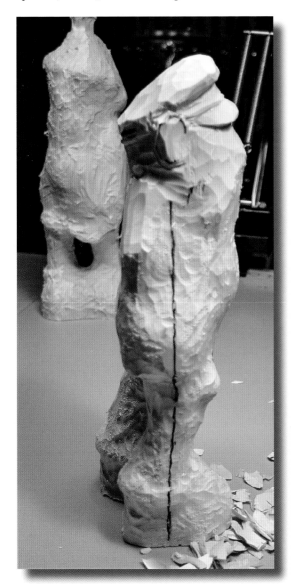

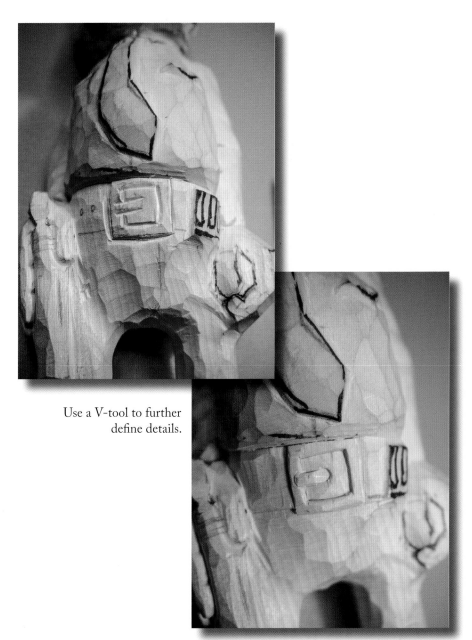

## BODY

Use pencil or Sharpie marks on the body to refine the shape.

Use a V-tool to further define details.

Try to think ahead to the next step, leaving wood for elements that will add some interest to the piece and prevent it from looking too flat or smooth. For this guy, that includes the badge, tie, pocket flaps and epaulets, bullets, and handcuff pouch.

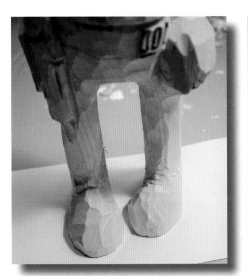  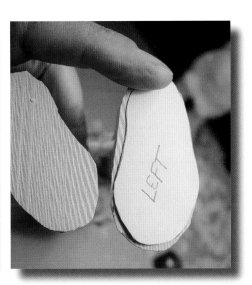 

**FEET:** Develop the foot until you're pleased with the size and shape. Trace around that foot and cut out the pattern, flip the pattern over, and trace it on the bottom of the unfinished foot. Using this trick keeps your carving from looking like it has two left feet. Using a V-tool, cut in the bottom of the pants and the sole of the boot. Add wrinkles to represent the creases in the boot.

 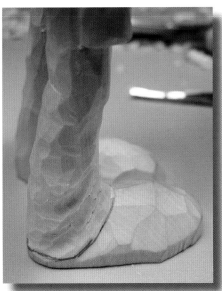 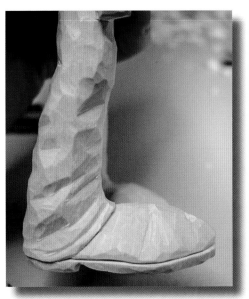 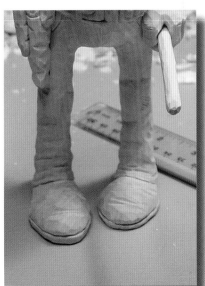

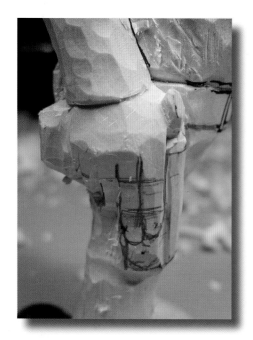

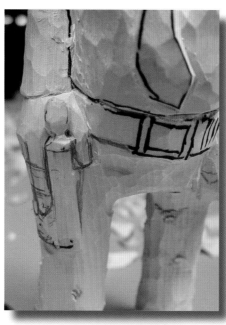

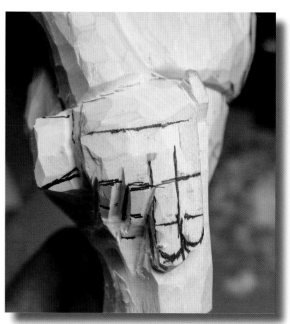

### RIGHT HAND

The first step is to draw the hand on the wood. Start with the index finger, separating the finger with a small V-tool.

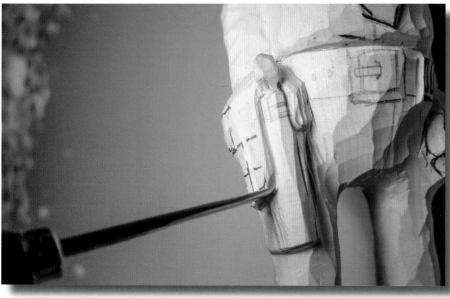

Use a small U-gouge to round the tips of the finger.

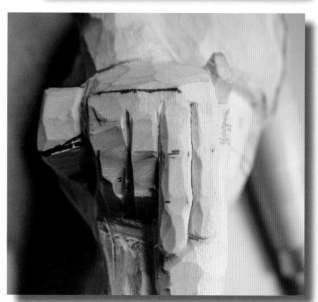

Shape the index finger with a knife and work toward the little finger, one finger at a time.

Not separating all 4 fingers initially allows for width adjustments as you move from finger to finger, leaving any additional wood to be removed after all fingers and the hand are shaped. Use a small V-tool for knuckles and fingernails, and a large #9 gouge to add detail to the back of the hand. Clean up any fuzzies and add detail and wrinkles.

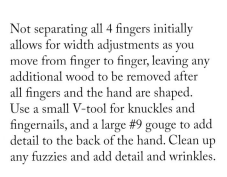

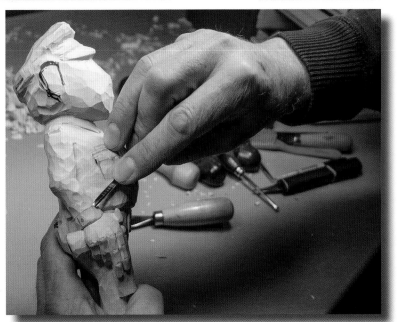

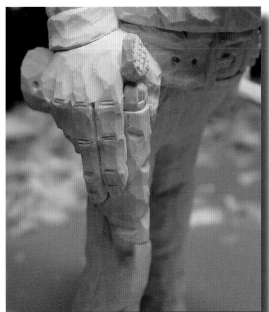

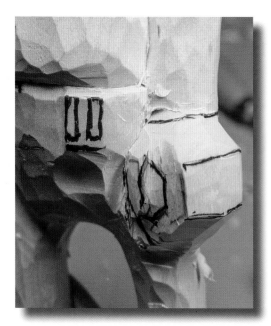

### LEFT HAND

Shape the left hand by using a wide #3 chisel or knife to develop the planes for the back of the hand and finger joints. Since the hand is gripping a nightstick, it also has some arc from front to back. As with the right hand, work from the index finger to the little finger, separating and adjusting the height of each finger.

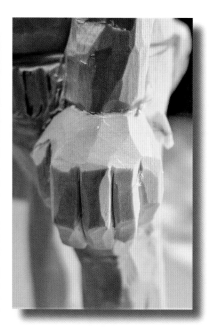

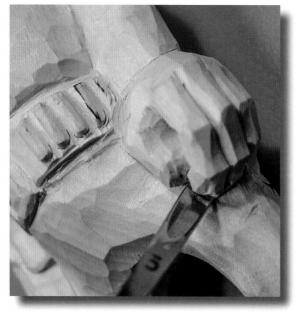

Shape the thumb and use a small, curved gouge to form the tips of the fingers. Use a small gouge and knife to make the opening in the hand fit the nightstick. On this carving I made the nightstick in two pieces: the long piece in the front and a small tip in the back. Add knuckle joints and fingernails.

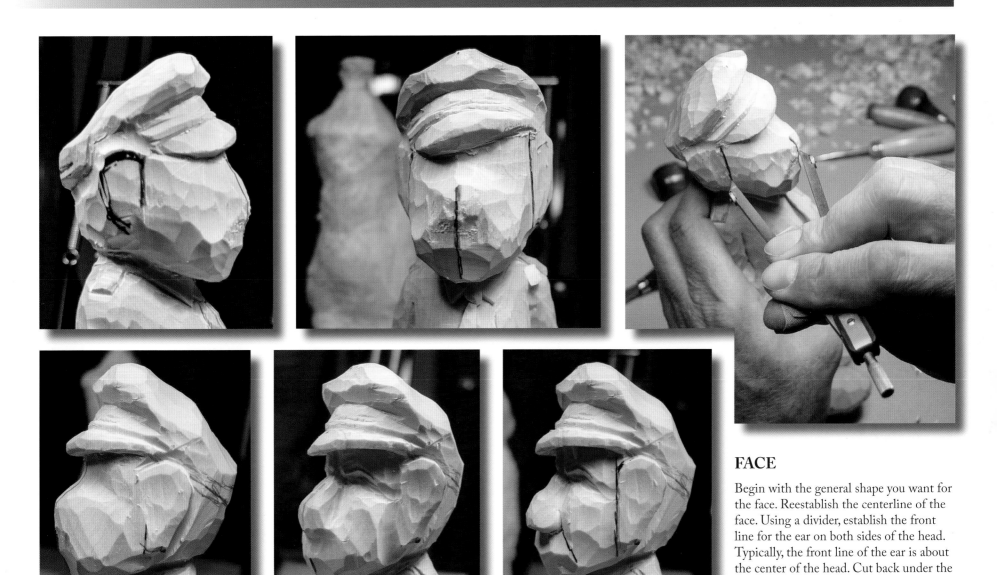

## FACE

Begin with the general shape you want for the face. Reestablish the centerline of the face. Using a divider, establish the front line for the ear on both sides of the head. Typically, the front line of the ear is about the center of the head. Cut back under the brim of the hat with a knife to form the bridge of the nose and brow line. Shape the nose, develop the eye pockets, and separate the ear from the face.

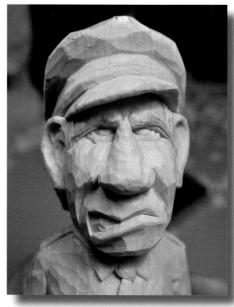

Using a knife, cut a deep line at the top of the eye, pencil in the eyeballs, and cut them in by using a small V-tool. Shape the mouth barrel. Cut along the side and bottom of the nose and relieve the V-shaped area to set the nose and establish the lines for the mouth. Cut in the mouth, lips, teeth, and nostrils, using a knife. Add wrinkles to the face by using a knife and #9 gouge, add the eyebrows and wrinkles around the eyes with a small V-tool, and use a U-gouge to add depth to the ear. Finally, detail the hair and hat by using a variety of V-tools.

In the end, it is important to take time to carefully detail the carving. Carve away any old pencil or marker lines, clean up any fuzzies, deepen cuts to add depth, and add more wrinkles. Chris Hammack once told me that he adds a wrinkle anywhere there's a straight line more than ½ inch long; it's a great rule of thumb for a caricature carving. And finally, in preparation for painting, wash the carving with Dawn dish soap on a hot, wet washcloth. It removes the dirt and oils that accumulate from being handled during carving, and will allow the paint to absorb evenly.

## EXTRAS

I think each carving tells a story, one hopes without requiring a title. For this piece, I added a couple of donuts to the nightstick, a backdrop with a donut sign, and a parking meter; all things associated with the police.

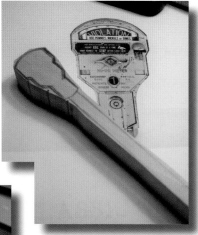

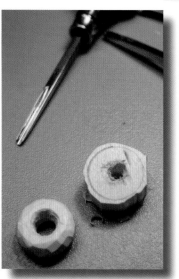

As I mentioned in the section on the left hand, the nightstick was added to the carving in two pieces. I also added a small rectangular name tag, because . . . despite my earlier suggestions, I forgot to leave wood for it in the roughout stage.

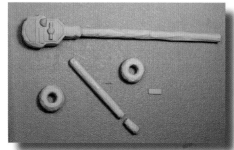

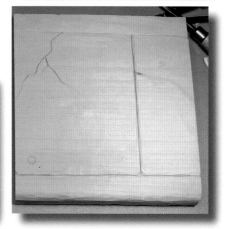

# PAINTING AND ANTIQUING

I paint using an acrylic wash. Principally, a little paint and a lot of water. I paint directly on the clean carving and do not use a sealer prior to painting. Place several drops of acrylic paint (6–7) in a paint tray and mix with water. Begin with the lightest colors first and progress to the darker colors. This process doesn't put a lot of paint on the carving, allowing the wood to show through. The antiquing step (described later) will bring out the color of the paint.

Blend colors while the paint is still damp or wet. The goal is to create variation in shade to skin tones, and to highlight wrinkles and transitions on your carving. While the carving is still damp, use a damp cotton rag to rub some of the paint away on the clothing, boots, hat, belt, etc. This technique highlights the tops of wrinkles and gives clothing and leather a worn look. Use heavier paint for details, such as patches, bullets, and badges.

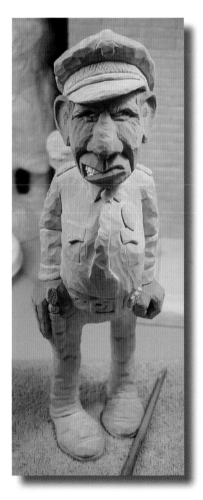   

Eyes are an exception to the painting rule. Paint the eye colors by using straight paint, forgoing the wash process. Paint the eyeball white. After it is completely dry, paint the iris (the colored part). Allow the iris to dry and add the pupil (the black dot). Outline the iris with a black line. Put a small, white dot on the edge of the pupil where it meets the iris. Finally, paint a thin black line on the bottom edge of the eyelid.

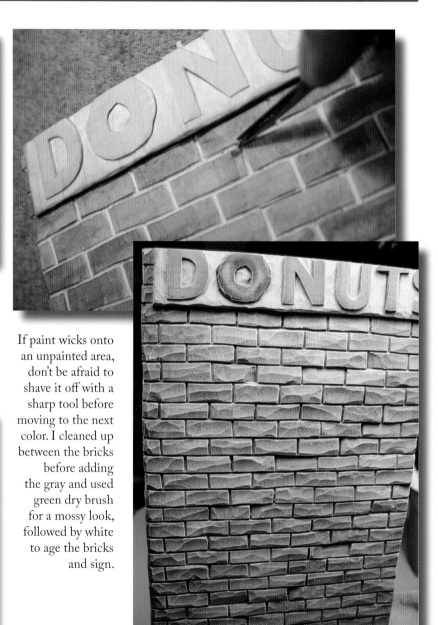

Use dry brushing to highlight hair, wrinkles, and the faceted cuts on the carving. Using a dry paintbrush, dip it in paint straight from the bottle. Wipe the paint off onto a rag or cloth. Brush across the carving very lightly with the brush until you see a very faint line on the top of the knife or tool cuts.

If paint wicks onto an unpainted area, don't be afraid to shave it off with a sharp tool before moving to the next color. I cleaned up between the bricks before adding the gray and used green dry brush for a mossy look, followed by white to age the bricks and sign.

After the paint is dry—usually overnight—antique and seal the carving by using a mixture of boiled linseed oil and brown oil-based paint. I use a mixture of burnt sienna and burnt umber, which looks something like liquid caramel. Use a disposable foam brush to paint the entire carving with the mixture. Let it stand for about 20–30 minutes and wipe it off with a soft cloth.

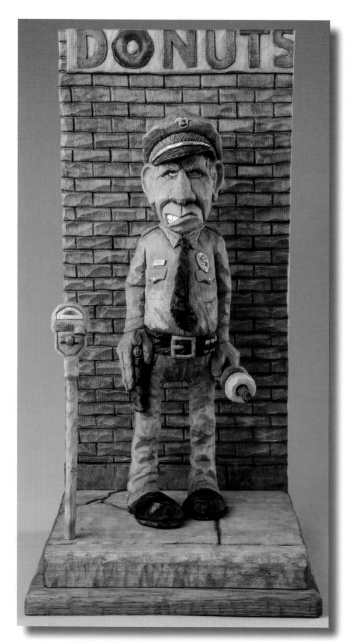

# Phil Bishop

Phil Bishop of Elk City, Oklahoma, was a full-time woodcarving instructor, along with his wife, Vicki, for eighteen years. He started carving in 1992, inspired by books by Steve Prescott, Cleve Taylor, Harold Enlow, and Tom Wolfe, and the fantastic carvings by Randy Landen and Dave Dunham. He also admires the cartoons of Herb Mignery and is taken with the creativity of Chris Hammack.

Phil began his teaching career with his first class in McAlister, Oklahoma. Then Ed Zinger gave him the opportunity to teach at the Woodcarving Rendezvous in Branson, Missouri, which gave him a shot for a very successful teaching career.

Phil and Vicki were on the road for about 200 days a year, teaching 25 to 30 seminars a year. They have retired from teaching on the woodcarving circuit and have sold their roughout business to CCA member Steve Brown. They are now creating one-of-a-kind singles and scenes for commission customers.

Phil became a member of the Caricature Carvers of America in 1998, an emeritus member in 2006, a member again in 2010, and finally emeritus in 2015.

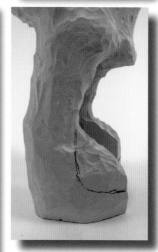

## *Harry Handler*

Now what do I want to carve? My wife, Vicki, carved a girl, Kitty Kartrashian (see photos in Members' Gallery). I carved a disheveled, sleazy, older man with a wrinkled suit, dirty shirt, and crooked loose tie, with glasses and a comb-over, to be her agent, Harry Handler.

This is a bulky roughout and, for me, has a lot of wood to be removed to get what I want, keeping its original form.

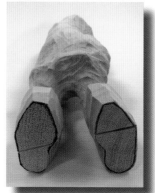

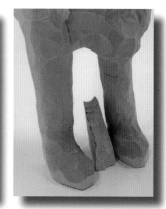

Draw a pattern for the feet on the base of the roughout and remove wood up to the pattern, saving a chunk for a cigar for later.

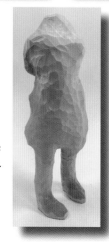

Draw the top of the shoe and remove wood from the top, making the legs longer and slimmer. Remove all roughout marks with a knife and a #9 ⅝" gouge.

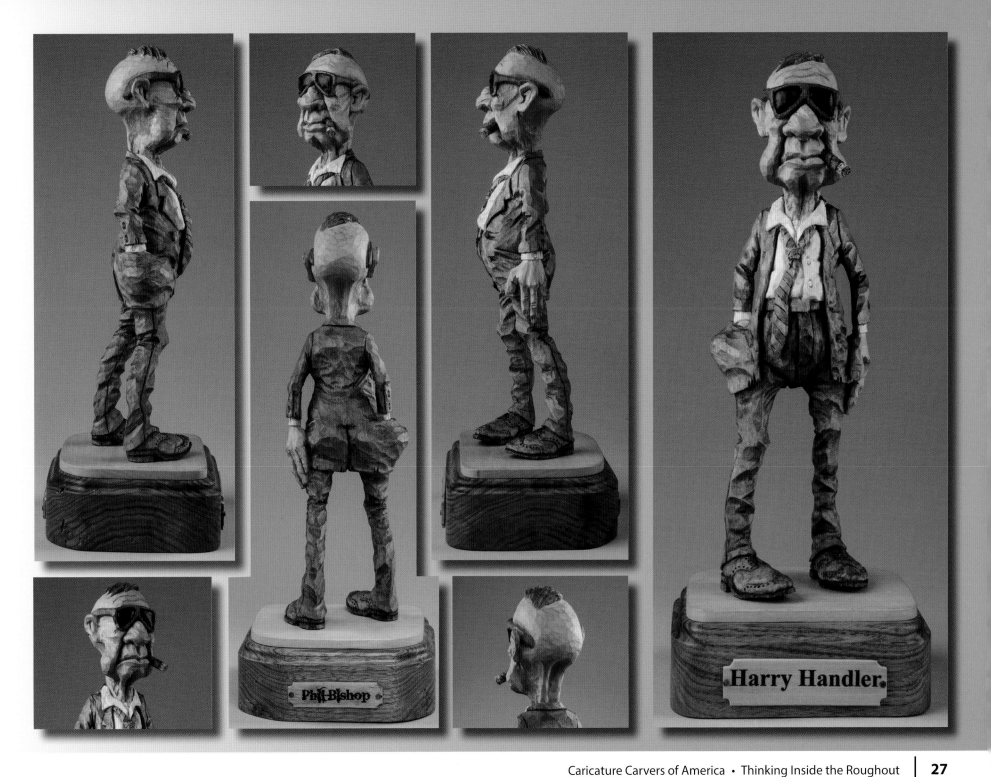

Phil Bishop

Harry Handler.

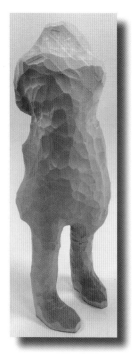

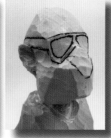

Shape the body for a suit, leaving wood for arms and legs. Carve the neck, creating the shoulders. Narrow the head down for a slim face. Round the top of the head to create an old bald head. Draw the ears and block them in. Carve the nose and flat part of the glasses on the front of the face. Carve the jaw line. Draw all the clothes, shirt, tie, jacket, pants, belt, and shoes. Draw his left hand and put the right hand in his coat pocket. Draw the comb-over and glasses. Use a ¼" V-tool to remove all the lines. Stop-cut all V-tool lines and relieve all of them. Undercut the relief lines to create shadows. Use a ¼" #11 gouge and ¼" V-tool to create wrinkles at the elbows, knees, and stretch creases. Detail the inside of the ears. Go over the entire carving, cleaning fuzzies and what I call shredded wheat. Using a pointed tip with a wood burner, burn the holes in the wing tips. Using a flat tip with a wood burner, burn strips on the tie. Use a ⅛" V-tool to texture the hair comb-over. Carve the mouth. Carve the cigar and insert it in the corner of the mouth. Add buttons to the shirt and jacket. Clean up all the fuzzies again.

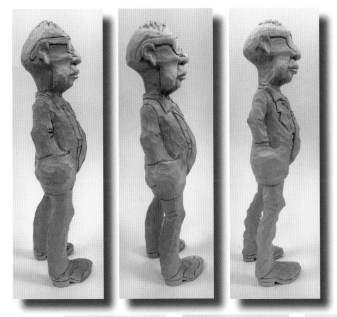

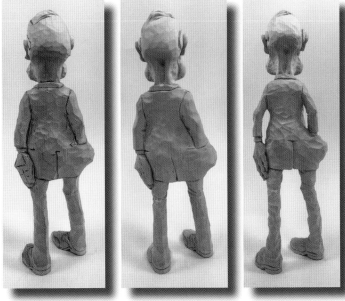

## Tips

- *Learn how to carve many different eyes and expressions. This will be more fun creating a story.*
- *Create action in all of your carvings.*
- *Try different styles of painting till you find one you like, to make you successful.*
- *Learn different techniques from several people you admire to create a style of your own.*
- *Have fun and enjoy the moment.*

# David Boone

David and his wife, Elaine, have always lived in Burnsville, North Carolina, which is the highest part of the Blue Ridge Mountains. Their ancestors settled here in the early 1800s. They have two children and five grandchildren who live next door. Their daughter has taught art at the high school for 26 years and owns an art and craft business. Their daughter-in-law makes pottery and works in the same shop with David. A grandson who is now a senior in high school has a business in wood turning and is beginning to carve.

During the past two years I have slowed on my carving due to arthritis in my hands. I did a special carving for the Southern Highlands Handicraft Guild that has been on exhibit this year in the Congressional Office Building in Washington, DC, a large (8 ft. × 6 ft.) caricature carving for Mayland Community College that is in the lobby, and a brown lab dog for the governor of North Carolina that is exhibited in the governor's mansion and the History Museum in Raleigh. Mount Mitchell celebrated its 100th Anniversary as a North Carolina State Park. I carved a bust of Prof. Elisha Mitchell, for whom the mountain is named, and a bust of Big Tom Wilson, who led a search that found Prof. Mitchell's body. Prof. Mitchell was an instructor at UNC in the early 1800s who measured the height of the mountain.

I have turned my art interest this year toward music. I have written many songs and made recordings in my studio. I enjoy playing all the different instruments, putting them on different tracks, bringing the music together with my song, and burning CDs. My friends seem to really enjoy my gift of CDs.

David Boone, 8659 Highway 197 South, Burnsville, NC 28714
Phone: 828-682-2838 • 828-208-0026
Email: eboone15@frontier.com

## Me Going Courting

The CCA members all received the same roughout. My first thought was "Shall I carve a cowboy?" I decided I wanted to carve something different that I had not carved before. When I carve, I like to tell a story. I want people to look at the carving and see if the person in the carving is happy or sad. Expression and feeling are important. Norman Rockwell was a master of this.

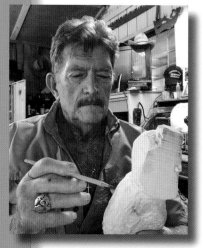

When I looked at the wood, I could see a boy or a caveman. I wanted to design something funny about a cave man. I had only one piece of wood. I decided why not carve a young cave boy? He would be dressed up in his finest clothing, with flowers in one hand and a club in the other hand. My title will be "Me Going Courting." He is off to find a young cave girl and take her back to his cave. The boy must look excited and his best, because this was a big day for him.

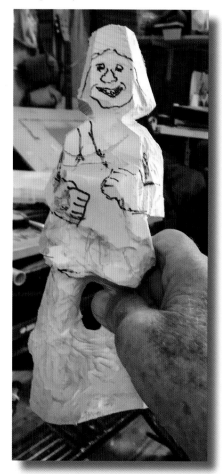

## Tips from David

• On the wood, I draw a rough sketch with a pencil.

• Rough out the carving as much as possible before carving detail. This makes the carving balanced and in proportion.

• On the bandsaw, cut away as much wood as possible.

• When the body of the carving is roughed out, then start working on the face.

# Steve Brown

Steve began carving in 1977–78 under the expertise of Harold Enlow. In 1986, he began traveling and teaching the art of caricature, carving along with judging competitions. Steve's various awards include overall best of Caricature Division at the Woodcarvers Congress, the Henry Taylor award, and 2nd Best of Show in the CCA competition. Steve was inducted into the Caricature Carvers of America in 2014.

Steve is the author of *Carving Pen Figures* and *Carving Figural Kaleidoscopes*. He organizes and manages the Renegade Woodcarvers Roundup, which occurs twice a year in Lebanon, Tennessee. He is a member of the Tri-State Woodcarvers Club in Evansville, Indiana; the Capital City Carvers Club of Tallahassee, Florida; the Atlanta Woodcarvers Club; the North Alabama Woodcarvers Association; the Emerald Coast Woodcarvers in Destin, Florida; and the Flora-Bama Cutups of Pensacola, Florida.

Steve is a native of Madisonville, Kentucky, and was in the healthcare industry for 27 years before retiring in 2003 and devoting all of his time to carving and teaching. He and his wife, Martha, relocated to Freeport, Florida, in 2014. They have 2 children and 7 grandchildren.

Visit Steve's website:
www.sbrownwoodcarving.com

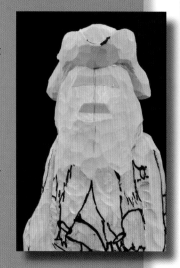

## Arrr . . . Matey

My first idea for this roughout was a Santa Claus. Then, as I looked to carve a second roughout, I wanted to use more of the wood in the head area. Thus, a Mountain Man with a ram's horn headdress was carved. I then carved a Pirate and decided to use it for my chapter because it had more detail to show.

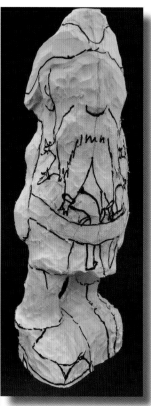
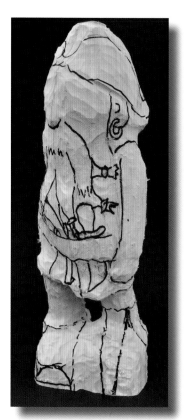
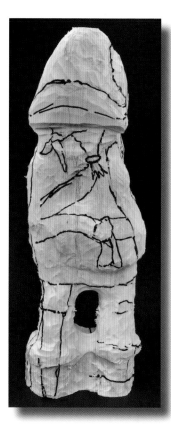

In the first few pictures, it shows all of the lines I drew in for the Pirate. However, please notice how I changed the lines or design as I carved the Pirate. A few examples of this are that I carved 2 earrings instead of one, removed the knife, moved the sash knot, changed the boot to a shoe, and did not include the shoulder belt. You may want to add an eye patch or remove a hand and carve a hook in its place.

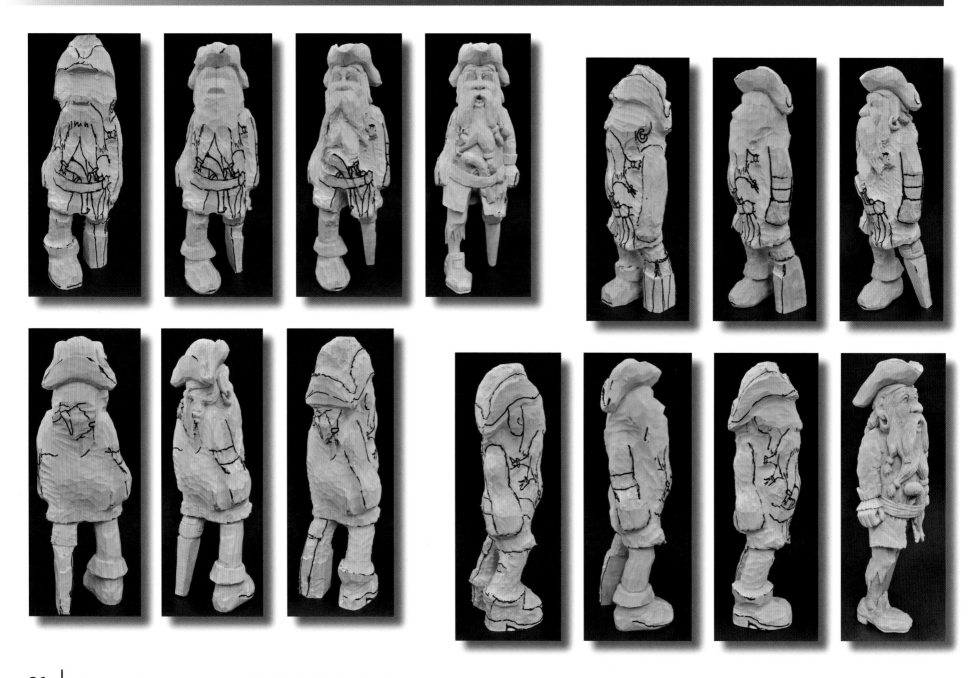

**Sealer:** I use Minwax natural stain/sealer before I paint.

**Deco Art Americana Paint colors:** All paints were thinned to a wash except where noted.

*Titanium white* – eyes, tooth, shirt, bandana, stripes for socks; dry brush on beard, coat, and pants

*Maroon* – hat, coat, blush on face, hands, lips, dots on bandana, stripes on socks

*Ebony black* – trim on hat, eyes, beard, hair, eyebrows, pants. All hair ties and sash have a thicker coat of black.

*Cocoa* – skin color

*Gold metallic* – trim on coat, earrings, tooth, buckle on shoes, buttons on coat sleeve, trim on gun

*Raw sienna* – pegleg, shoe (2 coats), wood on gun, thicker coat on eyes

*Neutral gray* – barrel of gun, nails on pegleg

Spray 2–3 coats of matte spray (any brand) after painting. After spray has dried, apply Deco Art Triple Thick to eyes, earrings, and gold tooth to give a gloss finish. Folk Art Antiquing medium is applied using a brush. I wipe it off with a damp paper towel, leaving antiquing where I think it looks best.

## Tips from Steve

*Carving from roughouts is a great way to get fast results in wood-carving. Although I sell roughouts, I recommend that you design and bandsaw some of your own patterns. Learn how to sharpen your tools and keep them sharp. It is so much easier to carve with a sharp tool. Don't forget to wear a carving glove. Try to get more people involved in woodcarving. It is truly a dying art!*
*Take a class with Steve:*
*Steve Brown, 85 Haven Way, Freeport, FL 32439*
*Phone: 270-871-4239*
*Email: sbrownwoodcarvin@bellsouth.net*
*Website: sbrownwoodcarving.com*

# Mitch Cartledge

Mitchell started carving in the early 1980s. His first carving was a pig carved as a gift for his sister.

His earlier interest in drawing cartoons eventually led to caricature carving, which he developed by studying books by Tom Wolfe and Harold Enlow. It was after meeting Tom that Mitchell joined the Charlotte Woodcarving Club in 1998. The camaraderie of the club energized him, but work slowed his development. It has been in the last twelve years that a move to Morganton, North Carolina, allowed Mitchell to devote consistent attention to carving, along with involvement in another club (Catawba Valley Woodcarving Club in Hickory, North Carolina).

In 2009, Mitchell was elected into the Caricature Carvers of America. Although he teaches on a limited schedule, since carving is still a hobby for Mitchell, he still works full time in the textile industry as a quality manager. He resides in Morganton with his wife, Page, who provides support and encouragement.

## Lost Bet

**Carving the Ballerina**

Many people bet on outcomes . . . sporting events, golf, bowling, cards, etc. Sometimes the wager is a little money, or wearing the opposing team's colors. This guy lost . . . well, a bit of dignity. But he got a new outfit in exchange! Not sure what the bet was about, but let's just be thankful that we don't have to watch the performance!

The lost bet resulted in our fellow dressing in a ballerina outfit, complete with a tiara. The pose suggests that he recognizes that he doesn't quite fit into the outfit—especially in certain areas.

He is relatively easy to carve. There aren't too many fine details, even though it is a relatively large carving. I generally go through the carving process in the following order: Rough out, Block out, and Detail. These are accomplished over the entire carving in that order.

Some of the illustrations are grouped by area (such as the face) and not necessarily in the order that they are carved.

I kept a mustache on the fellow—just to make sure that there wasn't any confusion about it being an ugly woman. I block this in with a ¼" #9. **TIP:** Use a larger flat gouge (½" #7) to narrow the face at the eyeline. This will help round the face and also push the cheek bones out.

Set the eye sockets with the ¼" #9 and make the area deeper at the bridge of the nose. Carve a small triangle above the eye at the bridge of the nose. This gives a shadow for contrast.

The upper eyelid is carved with a knife. Relieve underneath—carving the top section of the actual eyeball. Follow that up with the lower eyelid and finish cleaning up the eyeball. Be sure to clean up each corner. Add a few creases with the 3 mm #11 above the eye.

LOST BET

LOST BET

 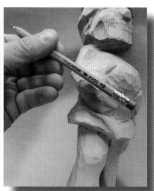

Use the soft V to block in where the arms and hands are to be located. Because he is grabbing his belly, I emphasize this with his thumbs extended upward. **TIP:** Use a straightedge to make sure that the alignment of the forefinger is parallel with the forearm. In this case, I used a pencil. For the finger separation I use the same technique: block in with a 3 mm #11. Use the knife to get clean separation between all areas.

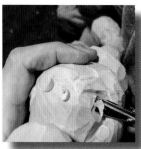 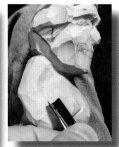   

 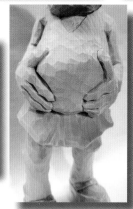

The top of the shirt is blocked in, and triangles are cut in each corner. Add knife cuts to connect the triangles to add definition between the shirt and chest. Hair is added with a small gouge, cutting shallow and across the grain. This basically covers the area at the top of the shirt, including chest hair, and a little on the tutu.

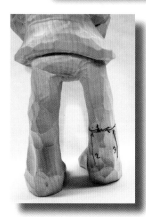 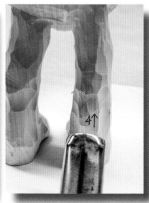

The calf is shaped with a #7 gouge. Cut number 1 is across grain to mark the top just below the crease behind the knee. The next two cuts are up and into the open area created by the first cut. The fourth cut is made by turning the gouge upside down and also cutting upward into the open area. This gives roundness to the calf.

Shape the legs with a knife all the way down to the ankles and feet. Get the feet close to the same size. For the slippers, make blocking cuts with a small gouge, basically using the tool to mark where the slippers go. Follow that up by first cutting shallow triangles in the corners with the knife, then connecting them with knife cuts in the deeper parts of the groove from the small gouge.

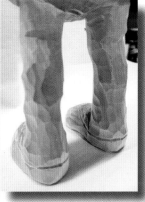
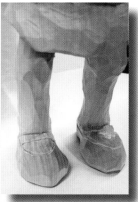

The tiara and hair are cut in with a small gouge and then further defined with a knife and V-tool. There is a deep triangle cut where the hair goes under the tiara band. This gives an ending point for the hair flow. Use short cuts with a ¼" #9 on the hair and then add further texture with a small V-tool. The tiara is blocked in with a 3 mm #11, then defined with a knife.

Wash the carving and paint the white on the eyes. Pretreat with Prestain wood conditioner after it has dried. The water-based version is easiest, and you can paint over it even if it's not dry. Paint with watered-down acrylics. Seal the carving with brushed-on oil-based satin lacquer—two coats. Antique with Walnut Gel-stain that has been thinned 50:50 with mineral spirits.

## Tips from Mitch

*Think about gouge cuts and triangle cuts as stop cuts and plan their placement when carving . . . especially when cutting with the direction of the grain. A well-placed end point will make a much-cleaner carving and also helps make the process go much quicker.*

# Ron Dowdy

Woodworking has been a lifelong vocation and avocation. Working with my father in a backyard woodshop and working summers in furniture factories while in high school led to a BS and MA in industrial arts, with a concentration in woods and a career in furniture production management. My free time was spent reproducing antique furniture, which introduced me to marquetry and some traditional carving.

All this changed in 1990, when I happened into Tom Wolfe's studio in Blowing Rock, North Carolina, and experienced, firsthand, Tom's style of caricature art. I immediately signed up for a class and have had a steady diet of carving classes ever since. I have been fortunate enough to work with some of the best carvers in caricature, realistic, chip, and relief, which have come together to define my own style of caricature.

Taking classes got me involved with different clubs, shows, and, most importantly, people with similar interest. While in North Carolina, I was a member of the Catawba Valley Woodcarvers in Hickory and NC Piedmont Woodcarvers in Statesville. Then, when my career dictated a move to Kansas, I joined the Great Plains Woodcarvers in Wichita for three years before moving to Illinois for four years. There was not a club near us in Illinois, but I was able to take part in some different shows and continue to take and teach some classes with a new community of carvers. In 2014, I retired and moved back home to Sanford, North Carolina, where I am active with the North Carolina Woodcarving Association.

In 2016, I received my biggest carving honor by being inducted into the CCA. While I have been fortunate enough to validate my progress by winning some top awards, the journey is the ultimate reward: new friends who creatively express themselves through their art, sharing concepts through teaching, and seeing people's approval through their smiles and chuckles.

Email: ronldowdy@yahoo.com • 919-770-3160

## Camp Cook

This project was not unlike carving "found wood," in that we were to use as many of the "humps and bumps" found on the roughout as possible. So, unlike most roughout carving, I began by "cleaning up" the roughout to see what stood out. Most apparent to me was a bearded man in an apron with something under his arm. I went with the obvious, and thus the Camp Cook was conceived.

After a little sketching, I started separating component parts. I found the feet to be two different sizes, so I evened them up and made them as large as possible. In caricature, we certainly have a creative license, and duty, to exaggerate different features, but they should be the same size. The same can be said for the arms: the length of the arms, or either half of the arm, can be exaggerated, but we should be careful to make the left and right arm the same size.

The butt seemed to have ample material, so I sketched in a knot for the apron on top of the belt and belt loops to offer a little more interest and a little more challenge. I was not concerned about any of the detail at this point, but I did want a reminder not to carve too much off when blocking in adjacent features.

The next decision was what is under the arm? A fat hen seemed appropriate for a camp cook, so I blocked it in. Finally, there was a hump of wood on the side of his face, which could either be a pet squirrel under his hat, carved off, or carved into a clump of unkept hair, which seemed more appropriate.

Now that the separate components were identified, it became a matter of "defining, refining, and detailing." I generally work all over a carving, rather than one component at a time. This allows for minor changes as the carving progresses. Larger components get attention first, since they may influence smaller details. The chicken has to be worked under the arm, which will dictate the size of the right hand, which will dictate the size of the left hand, which will determine the size of the axe handle. I continued to refine the different components until they looked balanced. The overall size of the right hand was blocked in, identifying where the hole for the axe handle would be.

There were two goals I wanted to accomplish when I put the axe handle in the hand: First, I wanted the hand tight around the handle; second, I wanted to be sure the handle was lined up straight from end to end, regardless of the angle it was being viewed. I accomplished this by drawing a guideline on the hand to establish the angle of the hole. Then, with a small bit, I drilled from both ends where the handle exits the hand. Then I connected the two exit holes with one continuous hole. (Any offset of the holes will be inside the hand and not seen.) The pilot hole is enlarged to the size of the dowel to be carved in the middle of the axe handle. When carving the axe handle, carve a dowel the diameter of the pilot hole in the middle of the handle, where the handle will be grasped by the hand. When the axe is complete, cut the dowel in half and fit the shoulder of the dowel to the contact point with the hand. Insert the two halves of the axe into the hand. I learned this technique from Peter Ortel and have found it an easy way to line up components held in a hand, such as an axe, a rifle, etc.

I continued to refine and clean up the carving, looking for unwanted stop cuts, fuzzies, etc. Then came the really fun part of adding details: knife slits in the beard to add depth, curls in the hair, wrinkles in skin and clothing, feathers on the chicken, distressing the apron and clothing, wedge in the top of the axe handle, fingernails, etc.

The face was laid out, being sure to keep the eyes perpendicular to the axis of the head to accent the tilt of the head. I continued refining the overall carving, including the apron knot on top of the belt. This is a detail that adds interest and is pretty easy to carve. Carve the apron knot and strings, then go a little deeper to show the belt and belt loops. Once all the exposed parts are visible, you can adjust the depth as needed to look believable. The internet is a good place to see the south end of a northbound chicken. The goal is not realism, but to convince the viewer it's a chicken—a pretty low bar.

One final addition is a base. I cut enough off the bottom of the roughout for a thin, simple base and still met the size requirements. I feel as though a base, even a simple base, is an important feature for a carving. It separates the carving from its surroundings, and if done correctly enhances the carving from a visual and compositional perspective.

It is said that "Some people paint to carve and others carve to paint." Regardless of where you stand on the issue, if you choose to paint, it is an important aspect of finishing the carving. I like to keep two things in mind when painting: First; I like to paint thin enough that the viewer knows he is looking at a piece of wood; second, I use only a few absolute colors. Most of the colors are blended or mixed, so it is seldom that I use a color right out of the bottle.

My painting technique is ever changing, since I try different things and experiment with tips from various teachers and see how they adapt. The basis for my painting is wet on wet with acrylics, as found in cheap bottles. The substrate is wet and the paint is thin. This allows me to build and blend color, making the finish more realistic. If done correctly, the viewer should not notice much of the shading, since it looks natural. However, compared to monochrome painting there is a vast difference in appearance.

My steps for painting include

- washing the carving with "Simple Green" or other liquid detergent
- mixing paint thin with water, sometimes cutting paint 400 to 500 percent
- after painting an area, wiping with wet cloth to remove some paint
- shading appropriate areas: folds, shadows, etc.
- drying
- dry brushing, sometimes for color, sometimes to accent facets
- spraying two coats of semigloss Deft, being sure to cover all areas
- drying
- using "bag" sand with crumpled kraft paper or paper bag
- antiquing with Liquid Watco Wax cut 3 parts natural to 1 part dark. Apply liberally, wipe off excess, let stand a few minutes, and wipe again, using a clean brush where needed to clean recesses. The wax finish can be buffed with a rag or brush for years to refresh.
- Do Not Set on Furniture till wax is completely dry or solvent will soften furniture finish.

I hope you find some of my techniques useful and enjoy coming up with your own designs.

# *Tips from Ron*

*If carving wood, don't hide the fact with paint. Be sure the viewer can tell the substrate is still wood.*

*When challenging yourself with a difficult project, take time to do some "easy" projects during the process to reduce the frustration level.*

*Experiment with different styles of carving (realistic, chip, relief, etc.) to see how they can be used to enhance your caricature carving.*

# PJ Driscoll

PJ began his love for carving in 1992. He was inspired by his good friend and coworker, Bill Jenkins. He has been a member of the Mid-America Woodcarvers since that time and has held numerous positions on the board. He is also involved in several woodcarving clubs around the country.

PJ was inducted into the CCA in 2008. He considers that to be one of the greatest achievements of his carving career. Since becoming a member, he has held the position of vice president and is currently serving as president. He has made numerous friendships throughout the CCA and feels very lucky to have met so many influential and interesting people. PJ is proud of the books that the CCA has published over the years. Some of his other achievements have been Second Best of Show–Peoples Choice CCA in 2004 and Best of Show CCA 2007. PJ has won Best of Show and has been a consistent blue-ribbon winner in the Mid-America woodcarving shows.

What started out to be a hobby has turned into something that PJ enjoys doing every day. He has shared his love for caricature carving by teaching woodcarving classes at Doane College for the last 20 years and teaching at numerous seminars throughout the country. In his travels, PJ has been an active judge at woodcarving shows. He looks forward to meeting all the different woodcarvers. He says he learns more by teaching, as well as taking classes. Developing your own style is the key to creativity.

PJ and his wife, Marge, have been married for 46 years, are both from Omaha, Nebraska, and have three children: Pat, Jeff, and Nicole. Their sons and son-in-law have followed in PJ's footsteps as Omaha firefighters.

PJ and Marge's greatest enjoyments are their children and grandchildren. Currently they have 6 grandsons and 4 granddaughters. They enjoy traveling, Nebraska football, College World Series, spending time together, working out, cooking, attending grandchildren's activities—baseball, hockey, soccer, basketball, gymnastics, and dance recitals—swimming with the family, and babysitting. They entertain friends and family with cookouts and pool parties. They enjoy holidays with their family. The children enjoy seeing what's new on the carving table. The family has seasonal favorites, such as Santa Clauses and Christmas ornaments.

## Hey, You Got a Match?

When the CCA came up with the idea of a universal roughout, I thought that would be a great project for a book. Considering the talents and imaginations of CCA members, it would be a great learning experience.

After looking at the roughout over and over again, I thought of a lot of things I could do, but the vision of a fireman kept coming up. The roughout was big enough to carve what I wanted. After sketching the idea on paper, I decided that I have carved enough firemen to proceed.

You have to go through the thought process before you start putting it into wood. I didn't feel I needed a clay model for this one. Dalmations, ropes, hoses, axes—all associated with the fire department—are things I tried incorporating in the carving. Many of my firemen carvings have told a story by being in a scene. This is a single carving of a fireman that has his hands full. From my experience in the fire department, when at a fire it never seemed like you could carry enough equipment. So that is why I loaded this fireman up with different gear. One of the things always said in the fire department when you saw someone loaded down with equipment was "Hey, you got a match?" That is the thought behind this carving. Roughouts limit what you can do, but this roughout gave me opportunity to express my ideas. This piece was carved with a sharp knife and a few gauges.

# PAINTING TECHNIQUES

Painting is something I like to do when I have a lot of time. It is not something you want to rush. I have thrown together a little bit of the painting techniques I have picked up from a few of my fellow carvers: Pete LeClair, Chris Hammack, Phil Bishop, and Dave Stetson. I like all of these carvers' finishing touches.

1. Make sure the carving is very clean. I scrub it with a toothbrush and Dawn detergent the night before. If you are in a hurry, forget this process.

2. I cover the whole carving with Minwax Natural Stain #209. You can purchase this at your local hardware store. The reason I do this is when you paint with watered-down acrylics, it doesn't let your paint run from one color to another. It is also very forgiving. If you make a mistake, you can use a water spray bottle to remove it. Whenever I am painting, I keep the carving wet.

3. I am not going to go into all the colors, but I usually use earth tones. Once in a while I will practice on a scrap piece of wood to see what the color looks like dried. If I like it, I use it.

4. After the carving is painted, I usually set it down and do a little touch-up wherever it needs it.

5. I seal the piece well with Deft semigloss. I use light coats of spray to make sure it is covered thoroughly.

6. My next step is antiquing. This process is the same one Chris Hammack uses in the CCA book *Concepts to Caricatures*.

7. I wax the carving with a dark paste wax.

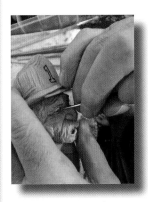

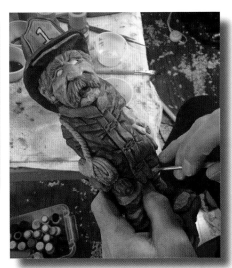

## Tips from PJ

- Learn to carve with a carving glove.
- Make sure you keep your tools sharp.
- Use a pencil to draw specific parts on the carving (arms, legs, etc.).
- Use reference pictures for your idea. You can find anything you want to carve on the internet.
- Take classes whenever possible; you will always learn something new.
- Have fun with it. Don't put pressure on yourself.
- Don't be afraid to try more-challenging carvings. That is what makes you better.
- Always be thinking one step ahead.
- Take your time, don't get in a rush, and always block your carving out first.
- Keep carving. The next one will always be better.

# Gary Falin

After 30 years of teaching troubled kids in an alternative high school, Gary retired 17 years ago to pursue the hobby he loves. He has been a carver for over 50 years and has taught for the last 35+ years. Gary is a versatile carver and has been a consistent blue-ribbon winner at the International Woodcarving Congress, Dayton Artistry in Wood Show, Dollywood, and others. He won a Second Best at Show at the first CCA National Caricature Competition in 2002 and was the Best of Show winner in the 2003 CCA Competition at Dollywood. Although he enjoyed competing, he has begun to focus more on teaching the art, with students locally, nationally, and traveling overseas for his classes.

Gary is a founding member and project leader in the Tennessee Carvers Guild. He says his style of carving has been greatly influenced by classes he has taken from Harold Enlow, Marv Kaisersatt, Dave Stetson, Gerald Sears, Claude Bolton, Eldon Humphreys, Pete LeClair, John Burke, Helen Gibson, and Phil and Vicki Bishop. He was elected to the CCA in 2004. Contact Gary at: 693 Wright Road, Alcoa, TN 37701.

## Elf Mountain Man

I like mountain men and elves, so why not combine them? This is an elf mountain man in a blanket coat with feathers and beadwork.

The carving was a little difficult because we were supposed to use the general shape of the roughout, not just carve away the wood to make a skinny carving. That's what I tried to do.

The features of the Elf are drawn on, the brow is cut with a ¼" #11, and the side and bottom of the nose are cut away with a knife. The nostril angles are marked and the grooves are cut with a ¼" #11. The back of the nostrils are cut with a ¼" #8. The arcs in the bottom of the nose are cut with a ⅜" #8 and rounded and shaped with a knife.

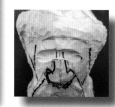

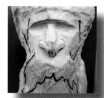

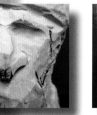

The eye sockets are deepened with a ¼" #11, the brows are separated with a ½" #8, and the sides of the face are drawn on. The sides of the face are cut with a ⅜" 60° V-tool and shaped with a knife. The ear is drawn and roughed in with a ⅜" V-tool. The top of the hat is established.

The centerline and outsides of the arms are drawn and roughed in with a ½" #8.

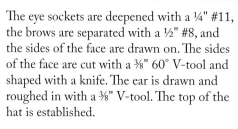
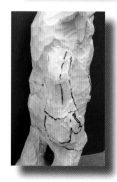
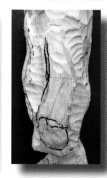

The bottom of the coat is established with a ⅜" V-tool.

The moccasin is roughed in with a ⅜" V-tool, then detailed with a V-tool and a knife.

 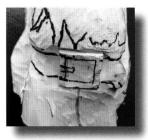 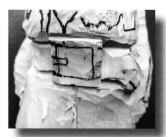   

The pants are shaped with a knife, and the belt area is roughly shaped with a ½" #8, leaving the buckle higher than the belt. The buckle is detailed with a knife. The bottoms of the sleeve and hand are drawn. The hand is roughed in with a knife.

    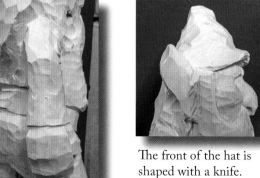  

The feathers on the hat are drawn and detailed with a V-tool.

The sleeves are roughed in and partially detailed with a knife.

The bottom of the hat is drawn in and cut with a V-tool.

The front of the hat is shaped with a knife. You can see the profile of the nose.

The ear and sideburns are detailed with a knife and V-tool.

   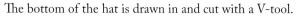   

The beard, mustache, and eyelids are drawn and detailed with a V-tool and knife. The feathers are detailed with a knife.

The hand is detailed with a ³⁄₁₆" 60° V-tool and knife.

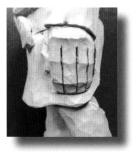

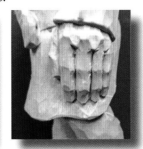

The beadwork on the moccasin, the buckle, and the lines on the coat are burned.

The carving is painted, then antiqued. After drying, the carving is sprayed with two coats of semigloss lacquer. After the lacquer dries, the eyeballs and buckle are painted with high-gloss clear acrylic.

## Tips from Gary

- *Spray your painted Santa beards, mustaches, or any large white area with alcohol or water. This will darken any missed spots, and you can touch them up before antiquing.*

- *When painting, keep a test piece of wood so you can get your colors right. Make sure you cut off saw or machine marks to simulate a carved area.*

- *When making stop cuts, make your first cut deeper than it needs to be. This usually makes the chip fall out cleanly with the second cut.*

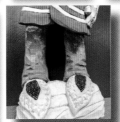

# Gene Fuller

Gene was born and raised in Nevada, where he graduated from the University of Nevada with a master's degree in biology, and went on to complete a PhD in zoology at Oregon State University. He spent the next 33 years as a member of the biology department at Boise State University, where he retired in 2000.

In 1998, he started carving at the suggestion of his wife, Jackie, who had purchased a starter tool set and a blank. She exclaimed that although the resulting Santa carving was "nice," she thought he should take a class. Thus began a journey that included classes and a close friendship with CCA members Cleve Taylor and Vic Otto, to whom he owes a great debt of gratitude, because this led to numerous classes from other CCA members and ultimately an invitation to become a member in 2005. During this tenure he was treasurer for four years, hosted the 2011 annual meeting in Boise, and contributed to five book projects. He was elected to emeritus status in 2016 and is pleased to be able to continue to contribute to the ongoing projects of the group.

He and Jackie live in Boise, Idaho, and have two adult children who live in Portland, Oregon. Gene is active in the Idaho Woodcarvers Guild and its activities, including the Idaho Artistry in Wood Show and Exhibition.

## Carving a Troll

### DEVELOPING A CARVING IDEA FROM A ROUGHOUT

A roughout is a carving produced by a replicating machine that carves away wood that outlines the original in a very general way. Most often the pattern and photos of the finished piece will accompany the roughout, leaving the detail work to the carver. The carver may elect to carve something very different from the initial idea, but with the limitations that arise from the wood removed. One approach is to make outlines—front and side—of the actual roughout, then construct a pattern within those boundaries. This is the approach used in the carving of a troll.

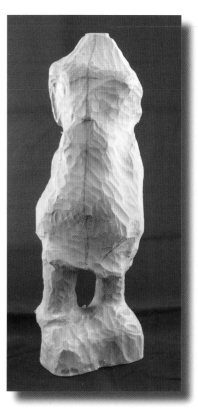

### WHY CARVE A TROLL?

There are many myths surrounding the origin and relationship of trolls to humans. They have been envisioned as monsters inhabiting swamps and woodlands, threatening humans who trespass. More recently, Norwegian trolls have become a tourist attraction and a profitable market. The Norwegian trolls have a rather distinctive humanlike form characterized by long tails, three fingers and a thumb, four toes, large eyes, a wide toothy grin, a long nose, and a short neck, all of which is quite adaptive to caricature carving and allows the carver considerable artistic license. They usually have expressions that represent a pleasant, joyful attitude, which, much like Buddha, suggest it is possible to be happy with very little.

The photo summary that accompanies this chapter was done with two things in mind. The first was to present photos of the carving in progress alongside a finished piece so that the reader could see how the roughout was modified.

The second was to present some possible modifications. For example, it is possible to carve the tail on either side of the figure; the other hand may be in a pocket, or it may be carved holding a walking stick; and finally, the troll may be carved without a hat, and the hat may not need to have a lizard sitting on it.

# Gene Fuller, *continued*

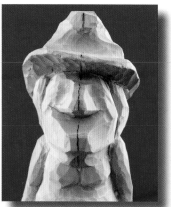

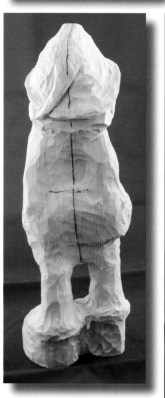

## CARVING THE ROUGHOUT

The first step in carving a roughout is to use a large gouge (#7 ⅜") to go over the entire piece and carefully remove all of the tool marks, being careful to preserve the basic form of the roughout. Tool marks discovered during the final detailing process can be a major problem. Carefully draw in a centerline but take into account that the figure is rotated to its right at the waist. Take into account some areas where asymmetry needs to be considered. Draw in major features, such as shoulder positions, waist and pant line, nose and jaw locations, and so on.

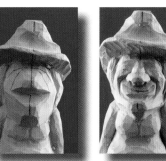

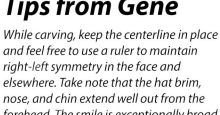

## Tips from Gene

*While carving, keep the centerline in place and feel free to use a ruler to maintain right-left symmetry in the face and elsewhere. Take note that the hat brim, nose, and chin extend well out from the forehead. The smile is exceptionally broad and extends into the smile line, so be sure to round the mouth area and narrow the chin so that it juts out. The teeth should be uneven, and three would be better than the four in the finished carving. The eyes are large and, rather than being elliptical, are very round. Another feature of the carving is that there is no neck, and the shoulders are rounded.*

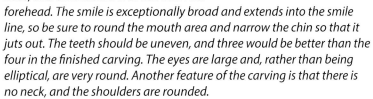

# Dale Green

Dale has always enjoyed dabbling in art, including drawing, painting, and sculpting. It wasn't until 1996 that he took his first woodcarving class, and he has been carving ever since. He quickly learned that his other artistic skills were valuable assets in carving. Dale has won numerous carving awards, including Best of Show 2012 and 2014 in the CCA's National Caricature Carving Competition. Dale was elected into the CCA in 2014 and currently serves as the organization's secretary.

Dale has designed a line of roughouts and enjoys teaching in his home shop and around the country. He is often heard telling others how carving has brought many new friends into his life.

Dale lives in Holladay, Utah, with his wife, Kerry, and their two dogs, Juno and Sadie. When he isn't carving, Dale is busy with art classes and playing the guitar.

Contact Dale through his website: www.dalegreenwoodcarving.com or email dalecarves@gmail.com

## *The Rodeo Queen*

Growing up in Utah, my family had a lot of fun at small town rodeos watching the locals try to make their ride. The rodeo always began by introducing the new rodeo queen and her attendants. Often rodeo royalty from years past would be introduced to loud applause from the crowd. I got to wondering just how far back in time they would go to bring out winners. That was how I came up with the "Rodeo Queen 1950."

When I first looked at the roughout, I wondered if I could get this old gal out of that piece of wood. As I began to draw a few lines on it, I could actually see the Queen in the piece of wood.

I began the carving process by marking lines to define the areas where wood needed to be removed. Once I had the lines drawn, I used a large V-tool to identify the major landmarks on the carving. Lay out the position of the arms and hands and the placement of the banner. Block in the face and the hair for both the front and the back, then begin to shape the legs and boots. This will give you the basic shape for the carving before starting work on the details. The next step was to remove the tool marks left by the roughout machine, to give me a nice, clean roughout to start the actual carving. With a large rough-in knife, I started to slowly carve in the major areas to bring out the final shape of the carving.

I carve with a couple of sharp knives, using both a rough-in knife and a carving knife. I also used a few tools on the project, including a couple of V-tools (large and small) and a set of small Dockyard gouges.

Decide the width of the Rodeo Queen's face and draw a centerline vertically, then mark the bottom of the nose. This will give you reference points for adding the eyes and mouth. To block in the hands, make sure you leave plenty of wood. Remember, it's always easier to take wood off than add it.

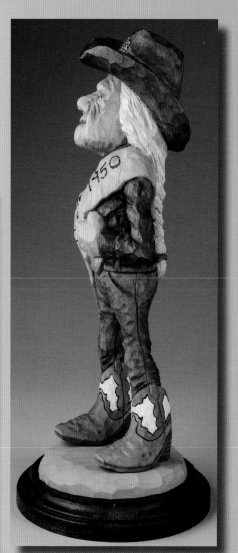

Braiding the hair can be a little tricky, but if you just start with a series of connected Xs you'll see the pattern start to develop. You may want to practice carving a few on a scrap piece of wood before putting it on your carving.

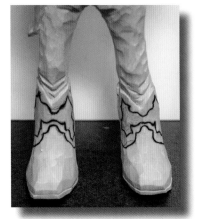  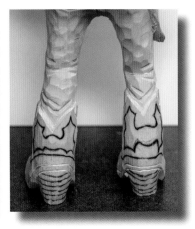  

To create a nice shadowing effect and keep paint colors from running into each other, I used a small skew wood-burning tip to outline the markings on the boots, tiara, and band around the hat.

Before painting, I clean the carving well with warm water and clear Simple Green to remove all the pencil and dirt marks left from carving. Once the carving is dry, I dip the entire project into a mixture of Watco Natural Danish Oil and a small amount of raw sienna oil paint, giving the carving a nice golden color.

I use acrylic paints thinned down to a wash so the grain of the wood will show through the color. When painting the tiara, I used a small stylus dipped into straight silver paint to follow the wood-burned lines on her hat. After the carving has dried completely, I use an antique solution of boiled linseed oil and burnt umber oil paint to set the colors and create the nice shadows on the carving. Let that dry for a couple of days before spraying the entire carving with a matte finish to protect the Rodeo Queen 1950.

## *Tips from Dale*

- *Don't rush your carving; remember, you're not in a race. You're creating a piece of art, and you want it to reflect your best efforts.*

- *Try your hand at drawing your own projects. Most of us don't think we can draw, but you'd be surprised if you give it a try. The real fun in carving is when you can create something yourself from an idea you've had or something you've seen. There are many internet sites for instruction on simple drawing techniques to get you started.*

- *Use clay to get your ideas into form. Clay is very forgiving and gives you a chance to try out different poses and positions. From there you can create your pattern. I use "Super Sculpy," but any clay will work.*

- *Most importantly, sharp, sharp tools. Nothing takes the fun out of carving faster than dull tools. And always use protective gear; a glove and a thumb guard at least.*

# Chris Hammack

My carving career began over 30 years ago. After an industrial accident, during a five-month convalescence, I picked up a piece of firewood and a pocket knife and began carving caricatures of the cowboys I sketched as a young boy growing up in Texas. Within two years, I began competing in carving competitions and even managed to win a few ribbons.

The years following would bring teaching a few woodcarving seminars and participating in several art shows around the country. While living in Colorado, I started a business called "Spit N' Whittle" that sold resin reproductions of my artwork that went around the globe. Subsequently I have also designed and sculpted several gift lines for other companies, and my work has been a part of Leanin' Tree Greeting Cards for over 25 years.

"I was told one couldn't make a living whittling. I'm proud to have proved you can."

Today, I'm happy to say I'm still carving. If you want to find me these days, you will need to go south of the border to a small island off the Yucatán Peninsula. You'll find me there sitting on the beach, third coconut tree from the sunset. I'll be holding a knife and a piece of wood, still trying to make somebody smile with my carvings.

## Crosscut

My good friend Kevin Kordtz from Colorado Springs is one of the finest caricaturists/cartoonists I have ever known. He always says "squint one eye and close the other, then see what it looks like." It is a great trick to help you look at something and get the overall gestalt of a thing without getting distracted by the details. This roughout was created by a committee of people adding bits and pieces here and there to an existing roughout so it could be basically carved into almost anything. So, when I received the roughout I decided I would use my buddy Kevin's eye-squinting trick and carve the first thing I saw. Well, maybe a psychologist might have a better one, but that's my explanation for the origins of Crosscut.

As for how to carve him, I guess the pictures mostly tell the story. I used a genuine Chris Hammack-autographed 1¾" flex blade, Helvie knife for 95% of the carving. For the other 5%, I used a ⅛" V-tool. My advice is to start at the beginning and keep carving until it looks like something, then quit carving. I tell my students in my classes to never be afraid to jump in and make the chips fly, because there isn't any mistake you might make that is so big that I won't sell you another roughout. I suppose the same applies to Crosscut. Try some special touches if you like. Earrings, bracelets, a cute spring dress, work gloves, an axe in his hand, just be creative. One touch I liked was the waffle grip soles on his high-heel shoes—"safety first" of course.

Never forget, the most important ingredient in a caricature carving is not action, or clean cuts, or a fine paint job. All of those can help, but the most important ingredient is always humor. A caricature carving without the humor is like a rum and coke without the rum. In other words, you might as well be a bird carver.

So have a little fun, and some laughs, and try carving Crosscut.

THE HAWG

THE HAWG

**Tip from Chris** · *Don't pick your nose and hold your carving knife with the same hand.*

# Bruce Henn

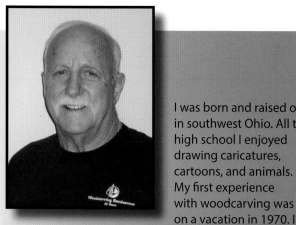

I was born and raised on a farm in southwest Ohio. All through high school I enjoyed drawing caricatures, cartoons, and animals. My first experience with woodcarving was on a vacation in 1970. I enjoyed it so much, I have been carving ever since. My first carving was a rabbit out of a redwood two by four (not a good choice), but that was my start.

My biggest honor of this carving journey was when I was voted into the CCA in 2006. I am proud to have served as vice president and president. I feel privileged to be in this group of fellow carvers. I have made many friends through woodcarving, and the fellowship means a great deal to me.

Over the years I have taken classes with close to 40 different instructors, a lot of whom were CCA members. I believe you never stop learning, so take a class whenever you can.

I started teaching woodcarving in 1981 and was asked to judge woodcarving several years later. I have enjoyed doing both ever since.

I am a member of the Dayton Woodcarving Guild of Dayton, Ohio; Brukner Woodcarvers of Troy, Ohio; Eastern Woodland Woodcarvers of Converse, Indiana; Muncie Woodcarvers of Muncie, Indiana; the Affiliated Woodcarvers Association of Maquoketa, Iowa; and the National Woodcarvers Association, as well as the Caricature Carvers of America.

## Chuck Wagon Cook

### "Carving the Roughout"

As I studied the universal roughout, I pictured a person with an apron on, like a baker, cook, et al. Since I like western figures, I decided to do a chuck wagon cook with a big mustache and a beard, since he has been out on the cattle drive for quite some time.

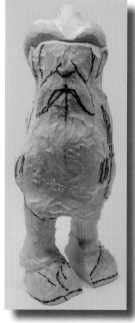

I started with a centerline down his face and outlined his mustache, the bottom of his hat, and his ears. These lines can be adjusted as you start to carve. I then bandsawed off his top knot and separated his feet.

Now I was ready to start carving. I began with the top of his hat and worked down to the face. After roughing in the hat, I roughed out the ears and sideburns. I like to start a face with these steps: ears, sideburns, and then the actual face. Then I roughed in the nose and mustache by using a ¼" V-tool to cut under the nose, and a ¼" #6

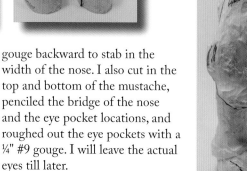

gouge backward to stab in the width of the nose. I also cut in the top and bottom of the mustache, penciled the bridge of the nose and the eye pocket locations, and roughed out the eye pockets with a ¼" #9 gouge. I will leave the actual eyes till later.

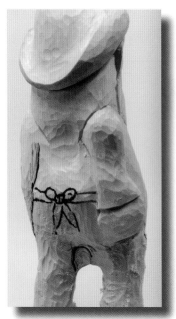

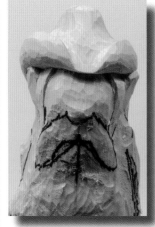

I started cutting in his hair and took it over his shoulders. His hair, being the same as his mustache and beard, is long and unkempt. I moved to his right arm and hand, cleaned up his apron, outlined it, and carved the bow in the back. I roughed in his left arm and hand, followed by the right leg and boot. Moving to his left leg and boot, I roughed them out also.

## "Time to Start Detailing"

I finished his legs, boots, and hands. I then worked on his mustache and mouth. I drew the top of his eye openings with a sideways lazy "S" and cut in the eyes with the tip of my knife (stop cuts and relieve to the stop cuts), followed by the bags under his eyes and eyebrows. I penciled in the irises to make the eyes stand out. I carved the inside of his ears and cut in the sideburns and hair with a couple of different-sized V-tools. I cleaned up all the fuzzies with my knife. Now he's ready to paint. I also carved a base for him to stand on.

## "Painting and Finishing"

I hold the carving under a bright light to see if I missed any area that needs to be addressed. If so, I do a final cleanup with my knife.

I use acrylic paint of various brands—whatever is on sale. I paint on the bare wood with light washes, then a second coat in the wrinkles and creases of his clothing to emphasize their lines. I then drybrush white on the high spots. After the paint dries, I antique the whole carving with a mixture of boiled linseed oil and a small amount of burnt umber oil paint.

**Note:** I did not paint his hat, since the antique mixture will give it a nice brown color that I like.

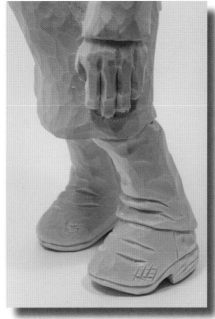

## *Tips from Bruce*

*I like to outline with a V-tool on the stop cuts so I can adjust the lines if needed. Once the lines are established to your liking, you can make deeper stop cuts on these lines to help stop your watered-down paints from bleeding across these lines. With the paints watered down, you can add additional paint coats to the detail for a shadow, or a darker look.*

*Strop your tools and knife before final details are carved. Learn to sharpen your knife and tools properly.*

*"Have fun carving."*

# Jim Hiser

Jim Hiser lives in Carlisle, Pennsylvania, with his wife, Joan, and works for a natural gas pipeline company in their telecommunications department.

Jim started carving in 2000, after attending his first woodcarving show in Mechanicsburg, Pennsylvania. He tried many styles of carving until taking his first caricature carving class with Peter Ortel. He immediately knew this was the style of carving he wanted to do. Always enjoying the humorous side of life, he found caricature carving allows him to express this. Jim has been fortunate to have carved with many of the top instructors in the country and believes in promoting caricature carving by displaying at shows and teaching. He feels there is no better praise than to see people smiling and laughing while looking at his carvings.

He is a member of the West Shore Woodcarvers, Mechanicsburg, Pennsylvania; Conewago Carvers in East Berlin, Pennsylvania; the Lancaster County Carvers, Lancaster, Pennsylvania; Eastern Woodland Carvers Club in Converse, Indiana; and the Pennsylvania Guild of Craftsman. Jim displays at woodcarving and art shows, winning Best of Shows, People's Choice, and Theme carving, along with many blue ribbons. His biggest achievement in carving is being inducted into the Caricature Carvers of America. Jim regularly demonstrates and judges at carvings shows and also teaches seminars around the country.

## *Santa*

When this project came about—take a generic roughout and carve whatever you want—I thought, "No problem, I do it all the time." Well, it did take some time to figure out what I wanted to carve. There was a lot of wood, which left many possibilities. In the end I decided to go with a Santa; after all, who doesn't like Santa? It seems that is one of the most requested carvings I get. With the project in mind, now how do I want to carve it? Will he have a hat? What are the hands doing? What types of footwear—boots, shoes, or slippers? What would Santa be doing? Looking at the roughout, it had the perfect setup for an apron, so I chose to put him in the workshop, getting ready for the big day, deciding to carve him holding a toy in one hand and paintbrushes in the other.

With this settled, I started marking up the roughout. I like a lot of guidelines before I start the blocking in phase because this gives me an idea on placement of the major components of the carving.

At this point it was time for a break and to get some ice cream. Chris Hammack and Don Mertz always told with me this is a very important part of designing woodcarvings and just makes life better. Who am I to argue with that?

With break time over, I started by removing wood around the head, moving my way down the carving, cleaning as I went. Moving back up to the head, I started carving the face, then laying in the hair, beard, and mustache. My initial carving had Santa with a full head of hair, but the more I looked at the piece, I chose to make him follicly challenged. Once satisfied with the head, I started blocking in the arms and hands, leaving extra wood for the brushes and toy elf.

The final phase of the carving was the detail, refining the shirt, apron, and belt. Working my way down to his feet, the shoes would have a buckle. Carving one shoe, then using it to size the second shoe.

Finishing up: I try to be a neat carver and make clean cuts, but it seems like I always have to go back and do plenty of cleanup. While doing this I'll add more detail if it is needed.

When I feel I'm finished, I set the carving aside for a day or so, then look it over to see if there is any adjustment needed.

As I looked at my carving, I didn't like the head from the side view—it was too wide. I proceeded to narrow the head from front to back and thin out the hair. Now satisfied with the finished piece, I scrubbed up the carving, removing any leftover pencil marks and oil from my hands. Now it's on to the paint table.

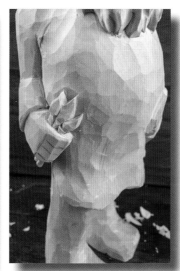

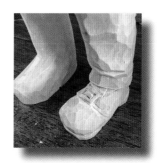
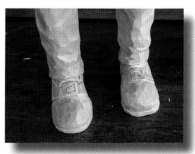

## *Tips from Jim*

- *Make sure your tools are sharp. It's safe and a lot more fun.*
- *Always strop your knife before you carve eyes.*
- *Take classes, no matter how long you have been carving. You can always learn something from others.*
- *Use centerlines.*

# Wayne Laramore

Wayne Laramore is a retired mental health administrator from Chester Mental Health Hospital.

His interest in carving began after attending class at Belleville Holzschnitzers carving seminar. At this event he had the pleasure of meeting Joe Wannamaker.

Wayne began experimenting with various woodcarving techniques and styles. He was introduced to Phil and Vicki Bishop after they presented at a seminar. He thoroughly enjoyed this style of carving. He draws from years in the retail store business and his time in the mental health field to create his caricatures.

Wayne is a guest carver at Silver Dollar City and Engler's Design Studio. He is also a long time member of the Belleville Holzschnitzers Club, where he serves as the treasurer.

Wayne was elected into the Caricature Carvers of America in 2016.

Wayne resides in Sparta with his wife, Pat. He is the father of two children: Amy (Tim) Price and Aaron (Shayna) Laramore; and four grandchildren: Will, Jake, Kaleb, and Addison.

## Fat Jack

The project was to create a carving out of a roughout. A lot of ideas came and went. After much considering, I saw a cook, or maybe a chef . . . Fatty's BBQ.

I made a few drawings of different caricatures and came up with a finished project. I drew an outline on the roughout before starting.

I try to carve in levels, removing wood from all areas as I work around the carving. I step back and look at the carving as I work. The details come last. Don't spend too much time in one spot. Make sure the proportions are pleasing to the eye.

Make clean cuts—no flat planes—since this will always help in the painting. Sharp tools are very important for making clean cuts.

Since the face is the first thing you observe, make sure the proportions are correct. Do the research; know what and whom you are trying to create. Knowing the proportions of a realistic head should help in carving a caricature head. If you have a sound base, you can be creative as you move forward. As you finish, step back and look at it from different angles. Before you paint, remove all burrs and flat surfaces.

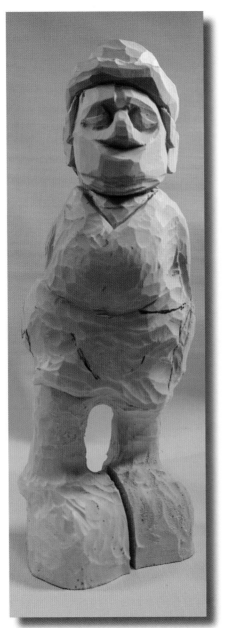

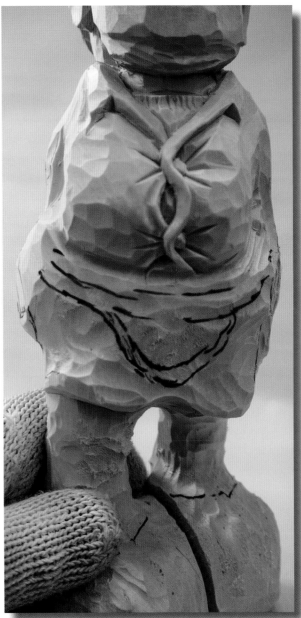

## Painting

The technique I use is watered-down acrylic paint. I seal my carvings with boiled linseed oil with a small amount of burnt sienna (oil base) mixed in. Painting it on and wiping off as much as I can, I often let it dry 12–24 hours. Soft tones seem to work best, letting the wood show through. Make thin, washed-out colors to create a better finish than heavy coats. I use a foam plate to put a drop of paint on, drawing it into a pool of water. This is done until I get the consistency I like.

I use 2–3 washes, then a darker color for shading, and then the original color watered down again for the final touch. On the face I let the wood show through and highlight with tomato spice and burnt sienna. Sometimes I dry brush a light color to bring the carving alive. This is done by using a dry brush and loading paint on it, then wiping off as much as you can, and then lightly brushing on to the raised surface. Very light; you just want to highlight this area. Now seal the carving with your choice of sealant. I don't antique my carvings, so if you choose to, you will have to paint the flesh tones before.

## Tips from Wayne

*Research your subject. Utilize the internet, books, and people watching. Knowledge will help for a successful carving. It's a good idea to work the piece up in clay or sketch different ideas out for a pattern. Enjoy what you carve . . . it will show in the finished piece. Have fun! Wear a glove! Take your time!*

### Painting

*I like the wood to show through on my carving. I use a light cover of linseed oil to seal my carving, wiping off as much as I can and then letting it dry.*

*I will use several washes of colors and then a darker color for shading. It's always better to use several washes than 1 heavy coat of paint. I prefer not to antique; it is just my preference.*

*Try different techniques until it fits your style.*

## A Funny Story

I'm the newest member of CCA (a great honor), so I am trying to get everything right for this project. My old camera was held together with duct tape and glue, so I'm headed out to buy a new camera. Now I'm ready to start and I took a lot of pictures, just knowing that everything was going well. The carving was nearly finished, so I was off to get the pictures printed. No pictures on the SD card to get developed; they are all in the camera's memory. After a few choice words and a trip to the camera shop, most of the pictures were retrieved. What a relief.

# Pete LeClair

I was born in Fitchburg, Massachusetts, in 1938, graduated from high school, then served four years in the US Navy. Upon discharge I attended Peterson School of Steam Engineering and received an operating engineering license. I worked in a large paper mill power plant for 38 years.

I have been carving since 1973 and began caricature carving after watching a local carver, Al Verdini, giving a caricature carving demonstration at a local shopping mall. I went to the local library to look for woodcarving books and found an Andy Anderson book, *How to Carve Characters in Wood*. I got so excited seeing Andy's humorous figures, I knew right then that's what I wanted to do. I've been a caricature carver ever since.

In 1990, I started teaching seminars in the Northeast. Since then, I have taught seminars throughout the United States, Canada, Wales, and Australia. It's been a heck of a ride.

In 1994, I was elected to the Caricature Carvers of America. Shortly after that I wrote my first book, *Carving Caricature Heads and Faces*, followed by *Carving Caricatures from Scratch* and *Carving Caricature Bust*, and I've participated in all CCA books (8).

Keep a sharp knife . . . Pete

**Note:** *I have a couple of videos on YouTube: one on painting and one on carving a bottle stopper head.*

**Painting Instructions Videos**

**Part 1:** *www.youtube.com/watch?v=cr0xzuriJi8*
**Part 2:** *www.youtube.com/watch?v=c2nBb4DxfmE*
**Part 3:** *www.youtube.com/watch?v=HAREx4YW7m0*

## Hobo

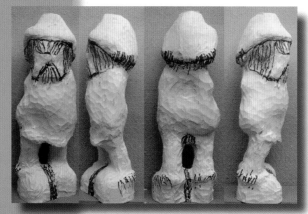

Mark the hat, face, hairlines, and shoe area and remove sharp edges. ▶

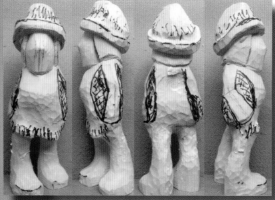

Shape the hat area. Round off the face, body, arms, and legs. Cut in the cuff and shoe area. ▶

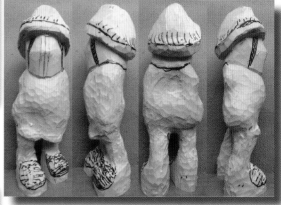

◀ Mark areas to be removed and then remove the wood.

◀ Remove more on the hat and thin the face. Draw in the front and rear of arms and the front of the shirt area.

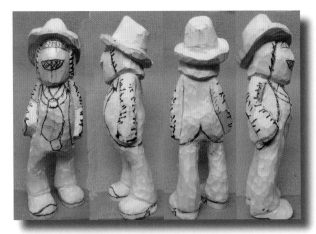

Mark in the eye area and the area below the nose, and mark all sharp edges on hair and arms. Draw in the shirt collar, neck tie, jacket, and shoe lines and cut and remove the wood.

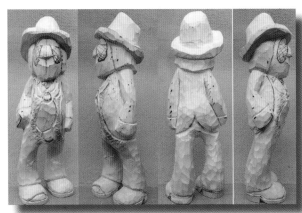

Shape the hat, draw in the area on the face to be scooped out, and V-cut all lines on the shirt, tie, and shoes.

Draw lines on the hat, draw the expression line on the face, and gouge out the area around the shirt, tie, and shoe area. Draw in lines on the hands, pants, and rope area and cut out.

Refine the hat and draw in the eyes, mouth, nostrils, details on the jacket, tie, fingers, and shoes, and cut in.

Cut in the eyes, nostrils, mouth, jacket, tie, and shoes.

Draw marks on the hat to make it look worn. Draw the area between the eyebrows, draw the eye area and draw the area below the lower lip, tie area, rope belt, button area, patches, and pant cuff area. Remove the shaded area.

Refine the hat, cut hair in, and draw the eyebrows and bags under the eyes, and then refine the clothes, belt, and shoe area.

Start at the top and work down, detailing patches, torn clothes, etc.

## *Tips from Pete*

*HAVE FUN. Try to find a local carving club. Carve safely, and carve with SHARP TOOLS and a GOOD CARVING GLOVE and THUMB PROTECTOR. I've found carvers are willing to SHARE, so ask an experienced carver for help in learning to sharpen your knives and gouges, and for carving help. Start with a simple project and work up from there. And when you feel good about your carvings, please help someone else get started.*

# Don Mertz

Don Mertz, a.k.a. the WOOD BEE CARVER, was inducted into CCA in 2009 and retired from active membership to become an emeritus member in 2017. He served as CCA secretary for six years. He publishes a blog *www.woodbeecarver.com*, as a journal of his carving activities, including instructional postings. Don participates in four carving shows in his home state of Ohio and teaches at the Ohio Buckeye Woodcarving Roundup in July each year. He is primarily a knife carver and has designed several carving knives under the Wood Bee Carver Signature Series knives made by HELVIE KNIVES. His motto, "Would be carvers would be carvers if they would carve wood," is meant to convey encouragement to all aspiring carvers to carve as often as possible, because "carving is a learning by doing activity" and "the more one carves the better one carves," so "Keep carving and carving will keep you carving."

## Windy Windale

"Caricature" is an exaggeration of realism. The CCA Universal Roughout project is exaggerated beyond any recognition of a specific subject, and thus this exaggerated roughout became a "caricature roughout" in its own self, awaiting the artist to set it free.

In the roughing-out process of removing wood chips, often the design will be dictated or come to life as chips are removed and the surface takes on a form of its own. This "design by carving" process changes the shape of the basic form by allowing the form to guide the development of the overall design.

The carving process is to encourage the development and growth of the skill of using tools in the carving process of shaping the wood. At the same time, latent creativity is awakened to see with imagination the carving tools shaping the wood in the mind before that message is sent to guide the hands to see the actual shaping of the wood.

Carving is a partnership between the mechanical skill in the act of carving (hands-on tool action) and the inner eye of creative imagination guiding the "hand and eye" coordination. To coin a phrase of this phase of creativity, "If it can be imagined, it can be."

Every carving project is a learning adventure of skill and imagination working together to develop the subject while allowing innovative shaping to happen during the carving process. Ninety percent of any carving project, whether it is a roughout or a block of wood, is to carve the basic form of the subject, with the final 10 percent used to carve in the details of the subject. The basic form is a silhouette image of the subject that will allow for a wide variety of detail designs to finish the final interpretation and presentation of the subject.

I am a knife carver who normally carves from a block of wood, making this CCA Universal Roughout project a challenge because of the random oddity of exaggerated shapes without any distinguishable subject design. The first stage was to visually study the exaggerated roughout with the inner eye of imagination to consider an appropriate subject design. Some areas of the exaggerated roughout had an excess of wood, while other areas had less wood, forcing the imagining process to explore various options. Finally, a cowboy theme was chosen, with guidelines drawn on the roughout as a map to guide the carving to basic form or silhouette image.

A variety of carving knives designed by this artist were used in carving first the overall basic form, and finally finishing with the detail carving. First the top of the hat was carved to basic form, then carving the head going up into the hat. This was followed by working down the rest of the cowboy by carving every area to the basic silhouetted form. This basic form carving helps keep the entire subject symmetrical by removing any optical illusions that would distract from the overall view.

Once the silhouette form of the cowboy was established to mirror the imagined mental image, the next step was to detail carve each area of the subject's form (i.e., boots, pistol, gun belt, hands, clothing, outfit, facial features, and minute embellishments).

Artist oil paint thinned with boiled linseed oil provided the finish coloring of the cowboy carving, mounted on a butternut base.

# Don Mertz, *continued*

Guidelines drawn on roughout to guide the roughing-out stage.

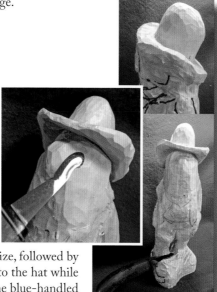

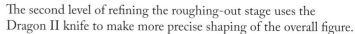

Carve the top of the hat to basic shape and size, followed by carving the basic form of the head going up into the hat while carving the bottom of the hat at the same time. The blue-handled Buzzard 2 knife was used for doing the roughing-out carving.

The second level of refining the roughing-out stage uses the Dragon II knife to make more precise shaping of the overall figure.

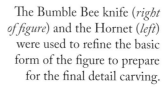

The roughing-out stage of carving to the basic form or the silhouette image of the cowboy has created a good foundation in which to begin detail carving the major areas of the figure.

The Bumble Bee knife (*right of figure*) and the Hornet (*left*) were used to refine the basic form of the figure to prepare for the final detail carving.

Detail carving of the hair begins with slice and roll cuts to form waves in the hair, followed by carving a representation of hair with a two-cut sequence for each hairline, using a perpendicular slicing cut, followed by an angled cut to the bottom of the first cut. A Little Stinker #2 detail knife was used to detail carve the hair.

The rest of the figure was detailed by carving in the facial features, the fingers on the hands, the six shooter and gun belt, the feather in the hat, the boots, and the bandanna. Two additional knives were used: a Viper 2 and a Green Hornet.

# Tips from Don

**Carving inside the box.** *Whether it is thinking inside the box or carving inside the box, it is helpful to think about the simplest definition for carving, such as "Rounding square corners and flattening round surfaces." When carving a ball in a carving project, be it a crystal ball for a wizard, a tennis ball, basketball, or a baseball, think of carving a square box on the outside of a circle a little larger than the intended ball. Once the approximate size of the box mirrors the size of a round ball, simply slice off the corners of the box to form a stop sign shape. Continue to slice away corners, making the octagon shape become a ball. The same "box" concept applies to carving hands first in a boxy shape, with angles and planes that give a silhouette image of the form of a hand. Next, round the corners by carving in the fingers within each angled plane of the three sections of the hand while carving the detail of the hand. This same "box" concept applies to carving shoes with a boxy form and then rounding the corners into the detailed shape of shoes. Remember that shoes do not sit flat on the floor but have a sense of movement, with the soles of the front of shoes angling up a little from the floor.*

**No straight lines.** *Carving is a "learn-by-doing activity," by being observant of the way things appear and by accepting the challenge to learn how to incorporate movement into the carving project with "S" lines in the form and shape of the carving. When carving a figure holding a walking stick or leaning on a cane, it is easier to intentionally carve a crooked stick rather than a straight stick. A straight stick is unattractive and takes away from the visual story of the subject being carved. A crooked stick is attractive in capturing the artistic eye with a sense of movement. It is like what a person sees while driving down a road lined with straight utility poles that are not really seen. On the other hand, if there are trees along the roadside, the eye will follow the crooked lines of the shape of a tree while overlooking the utility poles. Instead of carving a hand holding a crooked walking stick, some carvers will take the easy shortcut of drilling a hole in the hand and inserting a straight dowel rod through the hole to simulate the walking stick. That approach never looks natural and distracts from the artistic impression of the carved subject. Accept the challenge by carving the hand around a walking stick and carve a crooked walking stick to create the artistic "S" lines that are appealing to the eye. Whenever the "S" lines are incorporated in the pose of the subject, the folds and wrinkles of the clothing, the wavy shape of hair and beards, and the tilt and turn of the head, there is a sense of movement and life in a carving. No straight lines unless it is absolutely necessary, because a crooked line is always more interesting in its artistic appeal.*

**Carve every day.** *"Would be carvers would be carvers if they would carve wood" has been the motto of the WOOD BEE CARVER for more than 40 years. The meaning of this saying is "the more one carves, the better one carves" and "the only way one will learn to carve is to carve." Taking carving classes is an excellent way to speed up the learning process, but the better way is to intentionally carve as often as possible to "learn by doing." Even though a person may have other responsibilities, duties, and interests, doing a "20-minute-a-day workout" is a good way to keep the creative juices flowing. During these scheduled "20 minutes," one can take one carving tool and see what kind of cuts one can make in a block of wood. Doing so will make one very familiar with what that given tool can do, and even make discoveries of other ways to carve with that tool so that it becomes second nature without having to think how to use that tool. Another activity for this 20 minutes is to practice carving eyes, carving ears, carving the texture of hair, and making long and clean slicing cuts. Another 20-minute exercise is to practice shaping and sharpening a knife or carving tool. Nothing is ever lost with any of these practice activities, and even in trying a technique never attempted before. Two things will happen in these 20-minute exercises: the learning of new skills, and those 20 minutes expanding into hours with another carving project. Twenty minutes will take away that excuse that says, "I never have time to do any carving."*

# Ryan Olsen

Ryan Olsen began woodcarving while he was earning his master's degree in opera at the Cincinnati Conservatory of Music. He honed his skills carving in motel rooms while on the road performing opera professionally. He has studied with many of the greats, including Marv Kaisersatt, Dave Duhnam, Cleve Taylor, Chris Hammack, Phil and Vicki Bishop, and Dave Stetson. Ryan approaches carving the same way he approached learning to sing professionally: practice every single day and learn from the best. He enjoys the creative side of carving the most and likes the freedom of being able to carve what he wants when he wants. His advice to caricature carvers would be this: Slow down and do your homework. Push yourself to try new things. Carve what you know and don't waste your time carving cowboy hats.

Currently Ryan teaches high school choir and orchestra in Kuna, Idaho. He and his wife, Amy, have four children.

## Monday Morning Blues

As always, when I approached this project, I spent a great deal of time thinking about the character I wanted to carve. For years I performed opera professionally. I learned that to portray a character convincingly, I had to be very specific in my character choices. I use this same approach with my figures. Before I begin a carving, I answer questions such as these: How old is this person? How is he feeling at the time? What is his occupation? How is his fashion sense? What types of fabric is he wearing? How does he carry himself? Is he holding any props? As artists, we must be very specific. For many years I overlooked this preparation. I would look at a great caricature carving and just think that the carver was extremely talented. As I studied under these carvers, I discovered that they had spent a great deal of time researching and planning every aspect of the carving, including the wardrobe they would be carving, the nuance of posture, and the personality of the character. With a knowledge of all of this, the carving becomes much more specific and tells a much more interesting story.

For this carving, I decided to carve an exhausted working man at the beginning of another long week. He is getting ready for work, he hasn't shaved yet, and he is a bit strung out from the weekend. I decided to call it "Monday Morning Blues." I often feel this way when I have to drag myself out of bed after a late Sunday night carving session.

When I begin a carving from a roughout like this, I will generally draw a lot of guidelines to help define the shapes. When I am changing a roughout this much, I have to be very careful to maintain proportional relationships. I use the blade of the knife as a measuring stick and mark the spot on the blade with my thumb. I can then do a quick comparison. In these photos I am measuring the upper arm on both sides to make sure they are the same.

Ryan Olsen 2018

I decided I wanted to exaggerate the forehead on this character quite dramatically. The eyes are actually well below center. This creates a unique look. I always try to do things a little bit differently and to find my own unique niche or style.

I like to burnish the wood a bit with a wadded-up piece of printer paper. In painting this figure I used a light wash as always, painting the figure while it was still wet from scrubbing. I prefer to use my wife's favorite glass pie plate to mix the colors with water. I use a burnt sienna foundation followed by a medium flesh to achieve a natural flesh tone. I seal my carvings with boiled linseed oil unless I am experimenting with other finishes. My daughter paints with me almost every session. I have a box full of unpainted heads from my early days, and mistakes that she loves to paint right along with me step for step.

## Tips from Ryan

*If you want to carve people, there is no shortcut; you have to understand anatomy. You won't become great unless you supplement your skill set with things that don't involve a knife and wood. Take a figure-drawing class, learn to draw cartoons, sculpt, and become an appreciator of great caricature artists of all mediums. Take classes, read books, and watch videos. All of these things will seriously speed up your learning curve.*

# Pete Ortel

Before moving to Longs, South Carolina, in 2007, Peter Ortel was a New York native and resident, where he lived with his wife and family and worked as a firefighter. After 21 years of service, he retired from the NYC Fire Department.

He always had a talent for cartooning and had a desire to sculpt in wood and soon discovered that he could combine the two by specializing in carving caricatures. Peter found his passion and soon began competing in woodcarving shows and winning blue ribbons.

In 1992, he had the honor of being elected into the Caricature Carvers of America, an organization whose goal is to promote caricature carving as an accepted art form. He served as its president for two years, and after actively serving as a member for over ten years, he was awarded emeritus status and continues to participate in CCA activities and projects.

His most significant artistic accomplishment was to win Best of Show in 2000, at the prestigious International Woodcarvers Congress in Davenport, Iowa. Because it was the first time that a caricature won this award, it was considered a major breakthrough for caricature carving.

His most recent achievements were receiving the 2017 Best of Show award at the Annual Showcase of Woodcarvings in Charlotte, North Carolina, and second place in the 2017 Waccamaw Arts and Crafts Guild Annual Juried Exhibit in the Burroughs and Chapin Art Museum of Myrtle Beach.

Peter's work is in private collections and has been featured on television, in newspapers, and in national and international magazines. He is a member of several woodcarving groups, including the Charlotte Woodcarvers, the Cape Fear Woodcarvers, the Mid Hudson Woodcarvers Guild, the National Woodcarvers Association, and the Caricature Carvers of America.

He now enjoys teaching his craft, sharing his knowledge, competing and judging at woodcarving and art shows, and speaking about his favorite subject, woodcarving.

## Thinking and Carving Outside the Box

### INSPIRATION

Here's another fun project chosen by the members of the Caricature Carvers of America to inspire carvers and to help them get into a frame of mind to think outside the box and to execute those ideas into their carvings. Being a member of the CCA and surrounding myself with other carvers makes me strive to challenge myself and always keeps me on my toes. When each book project is discussed and chosen, so many ideas start to pop into my head, and I'm amazed at the variety of ideas from all the other members. Each idea doesn't always propel you to jump up and start carving it, but often one idea can start you down a path that may lead you to another idea and another, oftentimes as good as or maybe even better than the original idea (I hope the latter).

Well now, for me with this project . . . none of that happened. But I do believe we should surround ourselves with other carvers from all skill levels for inspiration. One of the questions I'm asked many, many times is, "Where do your ideas come from?" In response to that question, my answer is usually the same. "Anywhere and everywhere, from life itself."

For this project we were given the opportunity and challenge to create something different from a roughout that was kind of generic. Looking at the roughout that was chosen for everyone, my first vision was of a firefighter figure. (What else is new?) I needed to get out of my comfort zone. So there's the challenge. I needed to think outside the box.

The inspiration for my idea came from a recent trip my wife, Madelyn, and I made to visit lifelong friends who are living in New Mexico. It was a great visit, and so good to spend time with them again, but I didn't have my carving tools with me due to the fact that we were flying. To pass some time, I borrowed a book called *Don Quixote* by Miguel de Cervantes. I've loved the character Don Quixote ever since seeing the musical *The Man of La Mancha* in the sixties. He was the chivalrous, romantic, misguided hero of the story, and I had always wanted to carve him someday. So I put the fireman out of my head, and what started coming through was my old friend, Señor Don Quixote.

## CREATION

With sketch book and pencil in hand I went to work. Change this for that, move that over there instead of over here, take away some of this, and what do you know? He started to look like the Don Quixote figure I had in mind. Now I couldn't wait to get home to my studio to start carving. I had picked up a second roughout from the committee just in case. As you'll see from the accompanying photos, he started to come out, but the further I got into my Don Q, my inner self started to challenge me. Something was missing. Okay, I did need to add a sword and a lance. A horse could work, but I ruled it out. I still felt that something was missing. What could it be? Time to think outside the box a little more. I started to ask myself, "What would the Lone Ranger be without Tonto? . . . just another cowboy with a white horse. Batman without Robin? . . . certainly not the Dynamic Duo. And let's not even consider Roy Rogers without Dale Evans. I've got it! Don Quixote needs his faithful and practical squire, Sancho Panza. Well, I did have the extra roughout, but I don't know if the book committee would . . . ? Oh what the heck! My Don Quixote needed Sancho Panza!

## EXECUTION

"Okay Ortel, now let's make it work." Don was tall, thin, old, and frail. In his mind he was a knight in shining armor who tried, in an unrealistic way, to fight evil. In contrast, Sancho was younger, short, chubby, and down to earth. His practical common sense differed from the distorted realism of his master. I could envision all the above, but the challenge was to be able to execute two different-looking characters from one same-looking roughout.

Because the roughouts were a standard size, and Sancho was so much shorter than Don Q, I needed to rework one of the roughouts to allow for the difference. So what was the solution? Easy, I cut a chunk out from what would be Sancho's legs and glued the connecting pieces to disguise the cuts.

The accompanying photos should explain how I arrived at my finished characters, and I hope you're as pleased with the results as I am.

## Tips from Pete

*The best tip I continue to give starting carvers is to use a tool we take for granted—a pencil. Whether you're starting from a roughout or a block of wood, keep marking your work piece. As you carve, don't hesitate to change or alter your original idea as you work on it, and use your pencil to mark your changes. Things will pop into your design as you view your carving from different angles, and the pencil will tell you where to cut and where not to cut. Listen to it!*

*Using a small, stiff brush with liquid soap and warm water will clean off the smudges from the pencil marks on your carving.*

# Floyd Rhadigan

I started carving 48 years ago, after I came home from the service. I got hold of a book by Andy Anderson from an ad in *Mallet Magazine*. With the help of a family friend, Smokey Joe, I learned the basics: how to make a knife, how to keep it sharp, how to draw a pattern, and how use a bandsaw to cut it out.

I have carved all manner of things—animals, ducks, relief—but my true passion is for caricature carving. It was my great honor to become a member of the CCA in 2006, and to serve as president. Being a member is like being in a club where my heroes are members.

In 2016, I was chosen *Woodcarving Illustrated's* Woodcarver of the Year. I love what I do for a living; I plan to keep carving and teaching, and feeling blessed.

Contact me at: Floyd Rhadigan, PO Box 378, Clinton, MI 49236, (734) 649-3259, or email me at: rhads134@comcast.net, or visit my website: www.fantasycarving.com

## *Seafaring Pirate*

My first glance at the roughout, I knew I wanted to carve a Pirate. I have always had a fascination for pirates and seafaring people, from books, old movies, and television. The shape of the roughout threw me off a bit, with the feet pointing straight and body twisted and a shallow spot on the back, but there was plenty of wood on top for a large tricorn hat with a feather plume.

I always do research on a project. This is where Google Images and Wikipedia come in handy: the type of clothing and weapons used in that era, all that information at your finger tips. Attention to detail is very important.

So I started with a sketch of what I wanted to do and drew a few lines on the roughout. I was ready to carve. I generally start at the top and work my way down. I like carving the face first, since it helps me determine what I want to do with the rest of the piece; the fine detail I save for last.

Before I am ready to paint, I set the carving at a distance and look it over. If I need more depth or need to change anything, that is the time to do it.

I scrub the carving with dish soap and warm water, using a denture brush. Once it is dry I spray a light coat of Matte Finish Krylon #1311. This seals the carving and prevents the paint from bleeding together.

Now I am ready to paint; the paint brings the carving to life. I use thinned Jo Sojna acrylic paints for all background colors. On areas such as eyes, buttons, and belt buckles I don't thin the paint much at all. When I am done painting, I spray one more light coat of Krylon Matte Finish #1311.

My last step is to antique the carving with a mixture of 70 percent Watco Satin Finishing Wax (natural) and 30 percent oil base walnut stain. I brush it on, wipe it off, and buff it with a paper towel. **NOTE:** When using any product that contains linseed oil, saturate towels or rags with water before you dispose of them, because there is a chance of self combustion.

Now sit back and enjoy your work of art.

## *Tips from Floyd*

*If you want to become a good carver, you need to carve every day. In a year's time you will not believe how much you improve.*

*It is very important to research your project. The more you know about it, the better your carving will show detail, anatomy, and expertise.*

# Joe "Shoes" Schumacher

Joe became interested in woodcarving by watching carvers demonstrate their art in the early '70s in the Valley Road Woodcarving Shop at Silver Dollar City in Branson, Missouri. He began carving in 1990 and later joined the St. Louis Area Woodcarvers, the Belleville Holzschnitzers, and the Affiliated Woodcarvers Congress. He has taken over 120 classes, 28 of which were with past and present members of the CCA, and continues to learn to this day with clay, stone carving, caricature drawing, and other woodcarving classes. Joe became a member of the CCA in 2005.

## Reggae Singer

Dirty Harry once said "A man's got to know his limitations." To me that statement is the theme for this book. Instead of the usual idea of thinking outside the box, we are going to think inside the roughout. We usually start with an idea and develop a pattern for the piece, cut it out on a bandsaw, and carve it. Here we are starting from a generic roughout with limitations of size and shape, and we see what we can turn it into. We need to raise our creativity to counterbalance the limitation of size and shape. You could go into this project with a preset idea of what you are going to do and make it fit, but letting your creativity flow will let you see what it could be and not what it should be.

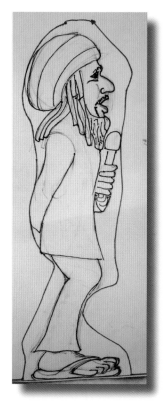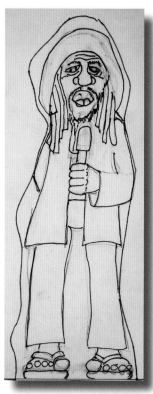

I had two roughouts to do, so I needed two ideas. I started looking at the roughout with my eyes and my hands. Your sense of touch can be a big help in the development of an idea. The **first carving idea** came to me as I looked at the roughout and saw a large amount of wood at one end, which I thought looked like a large mass of hair on a head. So I thought about types of characters with that look to them and came up with the Reggae Singer. On the sketches, you can see the red outline of the roughout to the front and side and how the drawing fits into it. I wanted a laid-back island feel to the carving: a cool breeze, a cold drink, and a good, mellow time.

For the **second carving idea**, I turned the world upside down—well, maybe just the roughout. Remember, you're looking to see what it could be. So the legs became the arms and head, and the large head mass became a . . . let me think on it for a bit. Hours later, and some cold drinks for a fresh perspective, and the head mass has become a . . . chair, that's it, that's the ticket, a chair with a guy standing on it. There, that wasn't so hard was it? (Note: The legs for the chair were added; everything else came from the roughout.)

# Joe "Shoes" Schumacher, *continued*

The Reggae man had the leg area already set, so I moved on to blocking out the body, arms, and head. I left plenty of wood for the head so I could alter the head position later on if I wanted to. You can see the progression of the carving in the photos. After the body, arms, and legs were complete, I started to refine the head. I wanted more of an easygoing look to him, so a little tilt to the head instead of a straight up-and-down look did the trick. After the carving was complete, I gave it a bath with mild soap and water to clean off any dirt or grime.

When I was finished, I came up with the idea of a scene for it to go into. A scene gives the carving a more finished appearance and adds to the story the carving is telling. After the carving and painting of the scene components, I assembled it. All done, I sent it out for pictures and a screen test. A star is born—well maybe a second banana. I hope you enjoy the book.

Later, when it was dry, I gave it a coat of boiled linseed oil. When it was dry to the touch I began painting it with watered-down acrylics.

## *Tips from Joe*

*Try different carving, painting, and finishing techniques from as many teachers as you can, so you can find the ones that fit you best. Carvers share better than anyone . . . ask lots of questions, keep a small notebook or sketchbook and pencil handy, and take photos with your phone; you never know when a great idea will come to you.*

*Before you buy a carving tool, be sure to try it out under carving conditions, not just on a scrap stick.*

# Sandy Smith

Sandy and her husband, Gary, reside in Lakeview, a small town in the Ozarks in north-central Arkansas. Sandy was inducted into the CCA in 2011 and stills feels honored to have been accepted as a member. She is the newsletter editor and webmaster of the North Arkansas Woodcarvers Club (NAWC) and cochairs the club's annual woodcarving show, a two-day woodcarving show and competition held annually in May at the Baxter County Fairgrounds in Mountain Home, Arkansas.

Caricature carving has opened many doors for Sandy, and she enjoys sharing her passion with fellow carvers. She teaches one-to-three-day seminars from her menagerie of "Critters," and although simple in design, nature provides an endless supply of subjects. What began as a few domestic dog and cat Critters for a single-day CCA carving class has grown to a minizoo plus a Santa. The final *Carving* magazine (Issue #45) featured a step-by-step of Santa, and *Woodcarving Illustrated* (Issue #74) carried a step-by-step of the Yorkie.

Sandy is honored to have been part of the production of the CCA book *Carving a 1930s Street Scene*. She designed and composed their previous book, *Concepts to Caricatures - Celebrating 25 Years of Caricature Carving*, and this book, *Thinking Inside the Roughout*.

Besides NAWC, Sandy is also currently a member of the National Woodcarvers Association and the Lakeview Carvers. She enjoys taking classes whenever possible and feels extremely lucky that Gary (and Augie, their cocker spaniel) travel with her for support at the annual CCA meetings.

## Well-Armed Bear

Carving a roughout is usually self-explanatory. It comes with plans or photos that show the carving's general form. Even though we were not told what the "original" finished carving to this roughout actually was, after my first glance I couldn't get the idea out of my thoughts that it looked like a fireman or a cowboy. I looked at the roughout from every angle and even moved it around the house, trying to "see something" in it. I laid it on its side, rotated it in every possible direction, and even turned it upside down to get the fireman or cowboy thought out of my head. I researched photos of children and adults and decided that since I'm most comfortable with carving animals, that was what I would focus on. Maybe I could carve two flamingoes, but the wood was not there for the bent legs. Maybe I could make it a meerkat because their legs are short and they stand up on their hind legs, but there was no wood for a tail. Only after making a "go-by" from clay did I finally come up with an idea. Bears have big heads, stocky bodies, and short legs, so I created a bear from the clay "roughout." Most of the images that I found on the internet of a standing bear showed the bear's arms out in front and dangling downward. This roughout did not allow me to do that, so I tried making the bear look as if he was flexing his muscles. I tried to make him a "well-armed bear."

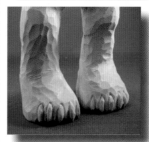

## Tips from Sandy

*Try something new—step out of your comfort zone. Attend as many classes as you can; you will always learn something new or a different way to approach a carving. Know where the cutting surface of your carving tool is, and make sure all body parts are behind it. Knowing where the point of your carving knife is at all times is the key to control. When carving, use a slicing motion to cut the wood fibers—do not just "push" your tool into the wood. Keep your tool edges honed for cleaner and safer cuts.*

# Dave Stetson

Criticism can have tremendous impact on an artist's level of development. In 1989, Dave met Steve Prescott and immediately began a relationship of camaraderie, love, and competition that eventually created the CCA. Their first meeting was documented in an article of the *Mallet*, where a carving trade appeared on the cover.

Dave and his wife, Michele, have been carving together since 1999 and critiquing each other's work even longer. Hence their development as artists has been a main goal since day one. Dave is rarely satisfied with his creations, always striving to add more movement and expression, or enhance the anatomy of his figures.

Dave has been carving caricatures since 1984, when he saw a carving show at the local mall and checked out a Bill Higgenbotham book from the library to carve "Cowpoke Charlie." There are exaggerated accounts of carving on his fourth-grade school desk with a new pocketknife that quickly became confiscated property of his teacher. However, he now creates caricatures based on exaggerated realism and is often referred to as one of the current masters of facial expression in wood.

He began teaching at the urging of Pearl and Cecil Wakefield in 1986. Dave's passion for imparting his knowledge of carving in his seminars is evident. His ambition is to excite carving neophytes to new heights of exploration on their own. He is willing to share every piece of information he has learned and to discover with those students who have the desire to learn. For those students who just want to finish a carving in a seminar, he will help you do that as well.

Dave has written numerous articles for *Woodcarving Illustrated* and a book for Fox Chapel Publishing, *Caricature Carving from Head to Toe*.

Dave's caricature is described as exaggerated realism and comes from extensive study of the human form. He teaches seminars and has judged carving and art shows all over the continental United States. While he is primarily a caricature carver, his artistic sense allows him to appreciate fine replications in all human, animal, bird, and fish forms.

## CCA Roughout Blank

Proportioning out the available wood for a standing figure, I'll start with the spine connecting the hips to the shoulders and see what's left for a head. I'll want to turn the head, raising the shoulder closest to the chin and lowering the hip under that shoulder, extending the foot under the lowered hip. The costume will consist of a suit and tie, with the fingers twiddling the tie a la Laurel and Hardy. I'll do as much as I can with the folds of material in the pants and jacket to fill in where there's plenty of leg and torso wood. The massive amount of head wood will allow for lots of hair. Still in the thought process, but sharing what goes on in my head when planning for a carving. Expression for a guy twiddling his tie would be kinda in line with a Stan Laurel smile . . . smiles always sell better than any other expression. Leave extra wood for large ears and plan out a hand and finger position with the tie. Maybe now would be a good time to watch an old Laurel and Hardy flick to make note of just how they flick that tie. Photos show the general preliminary layout views. Profile the face and create layout lines for the ears.

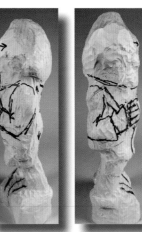

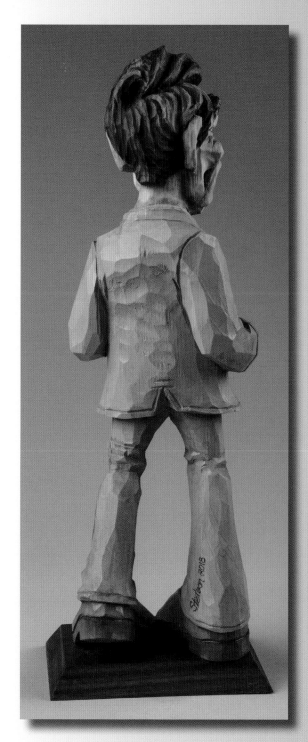

Cut in the ears, hairline, and arms. Try not to look at the head placement. Set the lower edge of the jacket, separate the legs, and lift the heel of the left leg. Lifting the heel of the foot is my solution to making the feet the same size; it also provides the illusion of movement. Lay out the tie, hands, and the jacket lapel.

Lay out marks for the eyes. Outline the lower half of the eye mounds. Mark the upper eyelid and nasolabial fold. Narrow the denture mound and set the upper eyelid. Cut in the nasolabial fold and mark the brow, eyes, and mouth. Cut in the mouth and lay out facial depressions for the jowels, chin, and brow. Cut in the jowels, chin, and brow. Define the eye pupil with pencil.

Lay out and set the hair track.

Saturate the carving with boiled linseed oil. Initial shading is with light washes of burnt sienna. Use light buttermilk for the eyes and teeth, sandstone for the shirt, and cadet grey for the suit; add charcoal for the shoes. Asphaltum for the hair, eyebrows, and the outside edge of the iris. Red for the tie. Cherry red for the tie highlight. Black plum wash for shading on the suit, shirt, tie, and shoes. Burnt sienna for the iris. Face closeup with burnt sienna for iris and hair highlights. Charcoal for the pupil, blush flesh wash for sunned skin tones, and light buttermilk for eye highlight. Also some buttermilk wash at the temples for whitening hair highlights.

# Dennis Thornton

Dennis has enjoyed working with wood and what he can create from it his entire life. As a young teen he began working with antiques, but he realized carving wood would offer him new opportunities.

In 1993, he first attended the American Woodcarving School, where he learned about woodcarving tools and wood. During and following this time, he began a long and very enjoyable process of taking classes with woodcarving instructors from all over the world.

Early on, Dennis developed an interest in all styles of woodcarving and has grown to enjoy caricatures. The emotion that one is able to create with caricatures is what he most enjoys and identifies with.

He belongs to many woodcarving groups and organizations around the country. He was honored in 1999 by being inducted into the Caricature Carvers of America and has served as president, vice president, and treasurer, and president again in 2018.

Dennis and his wife, Susan, live in New York, where their art studio is located. Today he continues to create new works, teaching around the world, exhibiting, participating in shows, selling his works, and repairing woodcarvings. As a recognized national painter, Susan also teaches woodcarvers the many ways woodcarvings can be finished. She specializes in working with acrylic paints and their effects when applied to wood. Their works have also been the subject of many publications and magazine articles.

Additionally, they are actively involved in conducting woodcarving and painting classes and seminars at their studio and aboard cruises around the world with Royal Caribbean, Celebrity, and Holland America Cruise Lines.

## Wise Old Owl

### The Challenge

A project to stretch your imagination, repurposing a roughout that was created to be something else. When I first inspected the roughout, I saw a cowboy, or perhaps a fireman, in the wood. I really enjoy this kind of challenge of examining the roughout provided in its entirety, and asking myself, "What else do I see?" As part of the challenge, the original purpose of the roughout was not disclosed. This enabled free-flowing thoughts on what could be pulled out of this block of wood without getting stuck on the original idea.

### The Process

When I was first beginning to carve, a mentor of mine, Pete Ortel, suggested I keep a concept journal by my side at all times. He explained that as a carver I was going to design carvings much quicker in my head than creating them with my hands. He advised me to start drawing and dating those ideas in a journal. I took his advice and since then have gathered hundreds of ideas and sketches. This was the perfect project to utilize one of those ideas. I came across the concept of the Owl. I have wanted to do this carving for a while. Expressing the mood of the owl drew me to creating this piece. I have found that in the world of caricature carving that different things make us all laugh and smile; however, some things are universally funny. When you see the opportunity for that in your piece you need to realize it and work with it. Not all birds really make me laugh, but owls are one of those I find comical. So I committed myself to try to figure out how to pull off this bird-brained idea.

When I researched the great horned owl, I thought the wispiness of its eyebrow feathers and its facial features could be stretched to create a humorous adaptation. I began to draw renditions of the owl and changed the features around his head. Next, I moved on to making an owl armature in clay so I could see a three-dimensional replica of my project. The armature process is valuable to make sure the wood for the body and perch would fit within the roughout wood parameters. It was easy now to transfer measurements to my blank roughout and begin carving.

# Dennis Thornton, *continued*

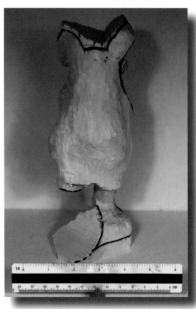

## The Rub

One would think that after all the research and planning, the carving would flow easily and be created in one attempt. As famed radio storyteller Paul Harvey would say, "Now for the rest of the story." Roughouts 1 and 2 bit the dust because I decided using the leg that stood forward as the owl's perch tilted him backward. It took roughout 3 to work the owl's tilt correctly. By roughout 4 I had finally worked out all of the kinks, which brought me to a finished carving I was pleased with . . . or so I thought. I decided to wash my phone with the laundry, which happened to have my photographic process of this project. Enter roughout 5, which allowed me to rephotograph my process. So after conceptualizing, research, clay armature, five roughouts, and one new iPhone later, I can sit back and smile at the completed Wise Old Owl.

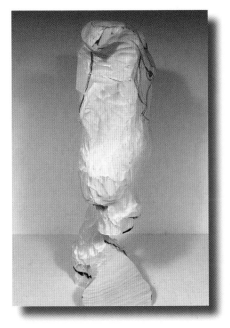

## *Tips from Dennis*

*Often I am asked this question regarding offering tips on carving. I quickly recite the same tips, since they tend to be as important every time I say them.*

- *Wear hand protection to keep from cutting yourself, a carving glove, tape, and an apron.*

- *Have a first-aid kit that is up to date, and consider updating an expired tetanus shot.*

- *Always use good wood.*

- *And always make sure all your tools are sharp at all times.*

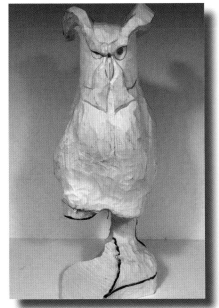

### Finishing Touches

I decided to texture the bark, using a wood-burning tip to get a realistic tree appearance and carved rocks at the base for the owl's perch. Next, using regular dish soap, water, and a toothbrush, I scrubbed the owl carving down, removing dirt, grease, and pencil marks to prepare the carving for paint. Using Jo Sonja's Acrylic Artist's Colours, Potting Shed, and Background Colours, the following paints were picked for the palette: Titanium White, Soft White, Smoked Pearl, Arylide Yellow, Yellow Oxide, Antique Brass, Carbon Black, Mouse, Burnt Umber, and Black Umber.

Upon completing the painting I allowed several days for the paint to dry completely and then sprayed it with Krylon Matte finish spray.

I believe carving is always a challenge, one I enjoy and like to share.

# Bob Travis

Bob is a founding member of the Caricature Carvers of America. He served two terms as president and was the project editor for our first six books.

Bob began carving in 1978. In 1982, while attending the Mid-America Doane Experience in Crete, Nebraska, he met Carlin Honaker, Bill Butterfield, and Mike Hawley. If you know those carvers, you will understand how he was soon hooked on caricature carving.

While caricature carving consumed much of his spare time, he also had a career in education. Bob retired as Professor Emeritus in Plant Science at the University of California, Davis, in 2005. After leaving his publish-or-perish life, he was able to devote more time to carving.

Teaching was one of his most enjoyable activities while on the faculty at UC Davis. The joy of interacting with students made the committee assignments, research grant and paper writing, and assorted unrewarding activities bearable. That same joy easily translated to woodcarving. Bob has taught caricature seminars throughout the country, including 25 years at the Doane Experience. He teaches caricature carving at the Northwest Carving Academy in Ellensburg, Washington, each July and frequently serves as a judge for carving competitions.

Bob and his wife, Mary, reside in Davis, California, during the winter months and in Montana during summers. At their age there are two things they refuse to do: live in 100-degree Davis summers and minus 40-degree Montana winters.

## *Confusion, the Rodeo Clown*

Old CONFUSION the rodeo clown. Somehow his elevator apparently stalled in the basement. At least we know it didn't go to the top. The BULL STOPS HERE might be his mantra, but his red flag appears to be yellow, and we all know that yellow means accelerate. Notice the look in his eyes. I think he just realized that the old bull is not going to stop. Maybe he should throw the white flag.

I'm not certain how the idea for this carving evolved. As you know by now, we all had the same blank for this project. The ledge about a third of the way from the bottom looked at first like the bottom of a coat. But then it also looked like the bottom of short pants. Upon further reflection, there was clearly enough wood on the top for a cowboy hat. So how about a cowboy wearing short pants? Probably not a good idea. What self-respecting cowboy ever wore short pants? Are you getting the picture? Of course, it had to be a rodeo clown.

My first attempt was a cowboy wearing short pants over long pants and cowboy boots. Not good for a rodeo clown, since long pants would cover the colorful socks that many rodeo clowns wear, and cowboy boots probably wouldn't work well when trying to keep bulls away from fallen cowboys. Although I've never tried running around a bull while wearing cowboy boots, I assume it wouldn't be a good idea. So I moved on to tennis shoes and colorful socks. An extended hand signaling the bull to stop would have been a nice addition, but the needed wood wasn't available.

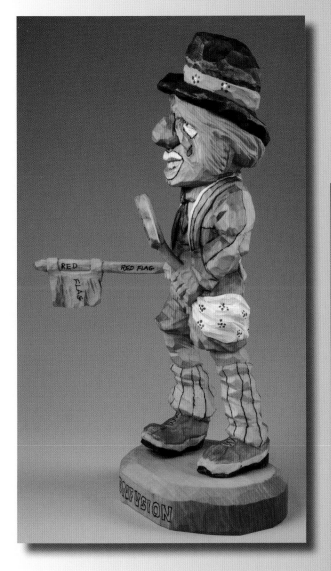

I prefer to block out the masses first. I draw a few lines to indicate arms, legs, and any major body or clothing masses. After blocking those in I begin to remove excess wood to attain the "personality" of the carving. For example, is he fat or thin? Is he standing upright, is he slouching, or is he bent at the waist? Next, I locate the joints in his arms and legs. After that, all that is required is to remove the wood that is not part of a rodeo clown.

Pay special attention to carving the face. Block the face in, following the example in the photos. The most important part of face carving is to form the rounded or angular sides on either side of the nose. This will alleviate the flat face that is often seen on beginner's carvings.

The lines on his suspenders, shirt, and socks were drawn with a black permanent-ink pen. I typically paint directly on the wood surface with light acrylic washes. Since this guy is a clown, I used stronger colors.

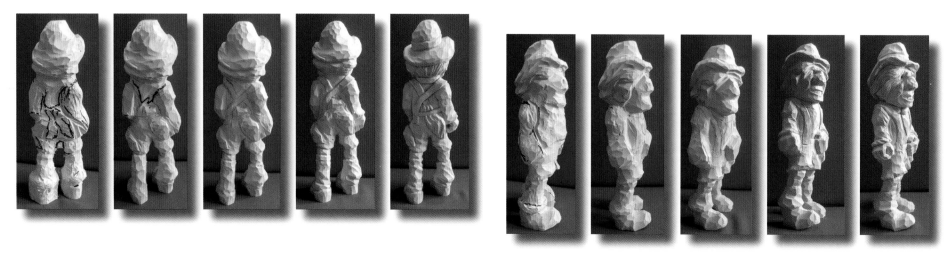

After painting it, I dipped the carving in linseed oil and added a light coat of Workable Fixatif spray. I hope you will try carving Confusion. The limited step-by-step photos accompanying the carving should be enough to get you through the process with little effort. Feel free to make him your own. An excellent resource for color photographs of rodeo clowns can be found by Googling rodeo clowns.

## Tips from Bob

*When attaching a carving to a base I prefer to use ⅛" wooden dowels. Some carvers use screws or metal pins. If a carving is placed under stress, the wooden dowels will break. If they break they can be replaced. Screws and metal pins will not break, but the carving may.*

*To repair a broken carving, apply a thin coat of carpenter's glue to both surfaces to be joined, then add a small drop of Super Glue. Move quickly when putting the pieces together, since you will have only 10 to 15 seconds before the Super Glue sets. Wait for the carpenter's glue to set before applying pressure to the break.*

# Rich Wetherbee

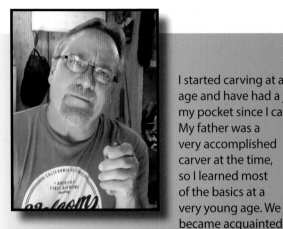

I started carving at a very early age and have had a jackknife in my pocket since I can remember. My father was a very accomplished carver at the time, so I learned most of the basics at a very young age. We became acquainted with the National Carvers Museum in Monument, Colorado, in the mid-'70s, and I really started to get hooked on woodcarving at that point. It was there that I met some of the more prominent carvers at that time, like Steve Prescott, Harold Enlow, Chris Hammack, Dave Stetson, Claude Bolton, and many others. I began doing art shows, displaying and selling my work throughout the US. Around the mid-'80s, I began Wetherbee Studio, where we would reproduce my pieces in molds and sell them to tourist traps throughout the country. At about the same time I joined up with a group of guys who had this great idea of starting an organization to promote the art of caricature carving, the CCA . . . thanks Dave and Steve!

I now reside in Colorado Springs, Colorado, where I have been since 1959 (you're doing the math, aren't you?). Mary Beth and I have traveled the US teaching woodcarving and sculpture, and enjoying all the great people we meet and all the awesome places our country has to offer!

Website: wetherbeecollectionllc.com

## Captain Robert Hook

This project was quite different as far as how I approached it. I usually design the piece in clay first and then do my woodcarving with that as my go by. In this case, I turned this thing backward, forward, and upside down, just hoping something would jump out at me (think outside the block), and it finally hit me. I've been wanting to do a pirate for quite some time, and what's a pirate without a parrot, hook, booze, and a bad leg! I named him after my nephew "Robert Hook"—he thought that was cool!

Woodcarving is a subtractive art form, so you have to think one step ahead of yourself . . . kinda like raising kids! I started by separating the Pirate's head from the parrot and shaping his hat so I could determine the head size. I decided on the placement of the nose, beard, and eye patch and moved on to shoulder height. I loosely drew in the arms and the parrot, and now I've got most of the outline for starting the upper body. I knew things had to become much skinnier to get the full roundness I needed for the arms, bottle, and parrot. Using as much of the roughout as possible, I carved in the sash, hook, and bottle. The legs seemed short at that point, so I bandsawed a lower foot line and used my mallet and chisels to get rid of the big stuff (so much quicker).

It's time to start forming the legs and sword; the tennis ball was artistic license! The rest was just putting in details. I really had fun with the parrot!

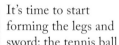

Although the tennis ball on the peg leg would have looked great in fluorescent green, I decided to go with a natural finish. I sprayed the carving several times with a clear matte enamel (Rust-Oleum) and finished it with a water-based antique (Americana staining antiquing medium mixed with a base color that would accent the basswood).

The project was challenging and fun! Can't wait to see what my partners in crime come up with! Happy carving!

## Tips from Rich

*I guess my biggest tip for intermediate and advanced carvers is to work your project out in clay first. Even if it's just a small rendering of your idea, it's a quick way to establish the gesture, movement, and proportions. I sculpt most of my projects to size and bake them so I have something to draw a pattern from and a go by to help me get closer to my original idea. I use Super Sculpey clay and bake it at 240 degrees. Most carvers have trouble drawing a pattern, so I think sketching in clay is a natural alternative.*

# Jack A Williams

Jack's carving started in 1973, inspired by a carving of an eagle plaque above a door at Disney World. The carving still has a special place on the wall. Jack knew he was destined to become a bird carver. For ten years he continued carving birds, taking classes and competing at the Ward World Wildfowl Competition. Jack moved on from birds to carving caricatures in 1988, after attending a workshop with CCA member Harold Enlow that changed his carving direction. Jack has studied carving with many great caricature teachers in the US and traditional carving in Austria.

Before retirement Jack was a professional photographer, which accounts for his interest and involvement in photographing woodcarvings for books and carving publications and competitions. Jack won first place in the Flex-Cut Tool Internet Carving Competition in 2001 and is a founding member of the Tennessee Carvers Guild. Jack has won a Best of Show at the Dayton Artistry in Wood Show, Peoples Choice and Best of Wood Sculpture at Dollywood, and Best of Division at the International Woodcarvers Congress. In 2002, Jack won a third Best of Show in the first CCA National Caricature Carving Competition and was selected to become a member of CCA in 2003. In 2003, Jack and Carole coordinated the Woodcarving Showcase at Dollywood and continued to do so for 15 years, and the CCA competition for four years while being held at Dollywood. Jack and Vic Hood were awarded the 2003 Independent Publisher Book Award, and in 2004, Jack was awarded the Ron Ryan Award from the Artistry in Wood Show in Dayton, Ohio. Jack grew up in Knoxville, Tennessee, and is now retired; he lives with his wife, Carole, in Sun City West, Arizona. His three children and seven grandchildren have claimed all of Jack's carvings, so that explains why Jack's carvings aren't for sale.

## Party Dude

When I first thought of this project of a carving from a generic roughout, I felt it might be a challenge for a creative group such as CCA. Speaking for this member, it certainly was. Bob Travis and I created this roughout at Bob's table at the Dayton Artistry in Wood Show. We

had asked Steve Brown to bring in a few of his roughouts that he sells to his classes. Bob and I then started adding Sculpey to the roughouts; thus the roughout in question was born. When the members received the finished roughouts, I began to look for ways to use all the bulges and all the dimensions. Out of the clear blue came the idea of a blue-collar guy getting dressed for a masquerade party as a cross-dressing dude. I should add that I have no experience in being a cross-dressing dude, so for the questions I had, I asked Google and found more answers than needed, and some that were too extreme even for a CCA book. What would he wear to a costume party? What style and color of wig? Where does one put their

tissue? What would he have in his hands, and what will they be doing? Also how can I position his arms to take advantage of the wood that makes up the roughout? My hope as you look at the roughout is you might see how I have utilized the wood. After the idea was born, I set out to make a model. After completing the model, I found it to be larger than the roughout, so when carving began I set out to adapt the features in the model to fit the wood. To make sure everyone can see the subject is a man, I put a shadow of a beard on his face.

The roughout can be purchased at the CCA Store on the CCA website, and you can take a stab at this project yourself.

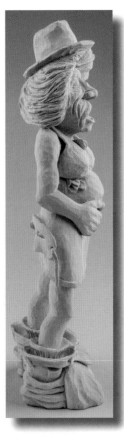

## Tips from Jack

*For me, the idea for a carving usually comes first, and then before touching a knife I dress in clothing that I have in mind for the carving and put myself in the position I envision. Prints are then made and then I can make my pattern. The Party Dude doesn't have on much in the way of clothing, but I didn't have any idea how to carve pants that have fallen to the floor. Taking my camera, we went out to the back porch, where the light is good, and I dropped my pants. Now you have to remember I live in a retirement community, and nothing surprises the neighbors. The picture showed exactly where the folds should be.*

*After the carving is completed and painted, I use Winsor & Newton "refined linseed oil," an artist-grade linseed oil bought from an art supply store. For the simple reason it is said that boiled linseed oil will yellow as it ages, whereas the refined artist grade will not, and it has far less odor. I add burnt sienna to the linseed oil for antiquing before the final clear spray of choice.*

# Tom Wolfe

Tom began carving at age 12. Today, he has become one of America's most recognized and respected carvers. A resident of West Jefferson, North Carolina, Tom has helped thousands of people develop their carving skills. In addition to teaching, he has written many books—more than 55 at last count. His approach to teaching through his books is straightforward. He leads the reader, step by step, through the carving process. His books have been well received from the newest learner to the most seasoned veteran because of the simple methods and obvious enjoyment Tom brings to his art. Tom sells his original work, as well as cast models and a series of cast characters he created for finer gift stores.

## *Blue Bucket Bill*

I'm often asked how I come up with ideas for a carving. For an original carving, I usually begin by sketching a few basic ideas. A few lines here and there, and then as the sketch evolves the figure will begin to appear. I began this approach years ago, when my son was a young boy. I would draw a squiggly line on paper and ask him to finish the drawing. Often the challenge included a specific objective. For example, I might ask him to draw a hillbilly, or a woman, or a cowboy, or an animal. Then we would reverse the process: he would draw the line and I would finish the drawing. Now that my son is older he is no longer interested in playing this game, but I still use the process when designing a carving.

This project required a slightly different approach, since we were asked to do a carving from a generic roughout. I decided early on to do a human caricature. Rather than beginning with a sketch, I sat and looked at the roughout for a couple of days. I was looking for some feature that would lead me into the carving. Maybe a hand or a leg. Perhaps an eye or a facial expression. Once I began carving, one part led me to the next, then further, and finally the carving appeared. In other words, as I worked I let the carving guide me through the process. This works for me about 90 percent of the time.

So how did old Blue Bucket Bill get his name? Like most folks in his world, he was branded with a nickname early in life. I don't think anybody knows his real name. But if you look closely you can see that he seems to be in a blue mood. With that, and the fact that his face is kind of bucket shaped, you can see how he got his nickname. Old Blue Bucket is a happy-go-lucky guy. He is one of those people who try hard, but never seem to find success. We all know somebody like that; in fact, I believe I went to school with Blue Bucket Bill.

The two female caricatures in the gallery were carved using the same approach. Red Hat Peggy began as a young girl dressing up to look like her mother, but looking kind of prissy. Then, as the carving evolved, she began to look older. Bad Mad Madge is either a bar floozie with too much makeup or Blue Bucket Bill's girlfriend.

# Tom Wolfe, *continued*

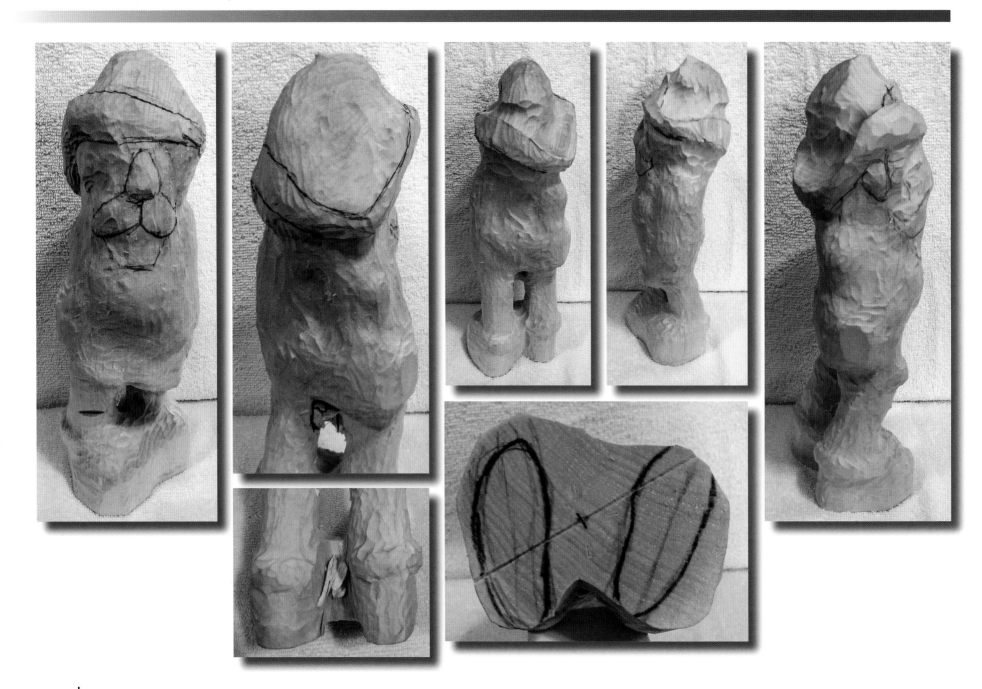

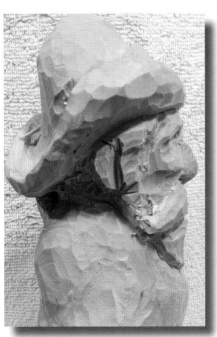

## Tips from Tom

*The only thing worse than not having a tool is having a dull tool. Dull tools will ruin your carving, so be sure to keep them sharp.*

# Joe You

Joe has always loved art and wood. He discovered woodcarving—especially caricature carving—in the early 1990s. Although he loves all things caricature, in recent years he has concentrated on faces. Carving wedding-cake toppers for his 3 children's weddings has been a highlight for him because it took all his skills to pull it off. He loves designing original pieces, mainly using a wire armature and clay. Joe has been a CCA member since 1999.

Joe and his wife, Chris, live in Sacramento, California. They are blessed with 3 incredible children and their spouses, and 5 precious grandchildren so far. He has been a practicing dentist for over 40 years.

## *Pirate and Friends*

What a fun and fascinating challenge it was to carve something new, unique, and creative out of a given roughout! This challenge is obviously

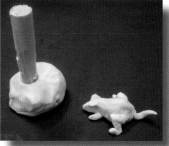

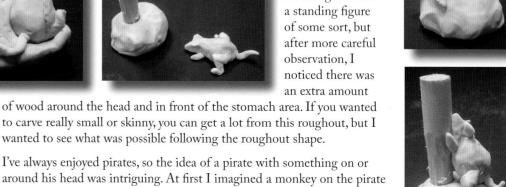

limited to the amount and location of wood in the roughout. At first glance it is a standing figure of some sort, but after more careful observation, I noticed there was an extra amount of wood around the head and in front of the stomach area. If you wanted to carve really small or skinny, you can get a lot from this roughout, but I wanted to see what was possible following the roughout shape.

I've always enjoyed pirates, so the idea of a pirate with something on or around his head was intriguing. At first I imagined a monkey on the pirate akin to Captain Jack Sparrow of *Pirates of the Caribbean.* But how would I fit the monkey in? Normally with an original carving I would work out a clay model, get a pattern from it, and bandsaw out the blank. Since I already had the roughout, I used the clay to help me design certain critical areas of the carving. After "monkeying around" with the clay, I came up with clay models for the monkey on the head, a hand holding the rat, the rat climbing up the peg leg, and the position of the open left hand. (See photos of clay models.)

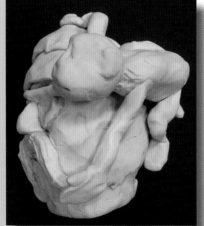

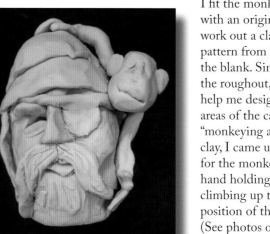

# Joe You, *continued*

The clay model showed me how the monkey was to be positioned on the pirate's head. This is not exactly the monkey I would have designed if I didn't have the limitations of a roughout, but it works. The extra wood in front, around the stomach, lent itself for the pirate to be holding something. After considering many objects that the pirate might have in hand, the finalist was a rat. It would complement the rat crawling up the peg leg, which I also did in clay first. I used Plastiline (oil based) clay to model these parts. Often I use Sculpey if I am modeling with a wire armature. If you are not sure how something lays out, it is really helpful to work from clay models. This will save you time and redos, and I believe it will improve your final carving.

Once you start carving and know where you are going, it is pretty straightforward. The most challenging, critical, and interesting part of carving something like this for me is roughing out. Getting all the shapes and forms for what's to come is essential. When you have all the shapes, forms, and contours done, only then do you think about details.

Painting is simple with watered-down acrylics (Delta Ceramcoat type). I always paint shadows by adding a little dark gray to the same color for shading in the creases, folds, and edges of the object. I like adding light ivory highlights with a dry brush. After the carving is dry I follow up with linseed oil and wax, either Watco Satin Wax or Clear Paste Wax.

## Tips from Joe

*Before any tool hits wood, plan out what you want to carve in your mind, on paper or using wires, pipe cleaners, or clay— whatever works for you. Your carving will go faster and there's a good chance it will be a better carving.*

*This is the time to decide on positions, placement, and form. They all help you determine what are the best positions of the head, back, hips, shoulders, arms, hands, feet, etc. Will they be slanted, tipped, turned, opened, closed, and so forth?*

*If a figure is holding something, should that object be higher or lower? Does it block something you want to see? You are the designer. Even clothes design should be worked out first.*

*I love working things out in clay—it is fun and fast. You would never build a house without plans. Carving an original piece is the same.*

# Members' Gallery

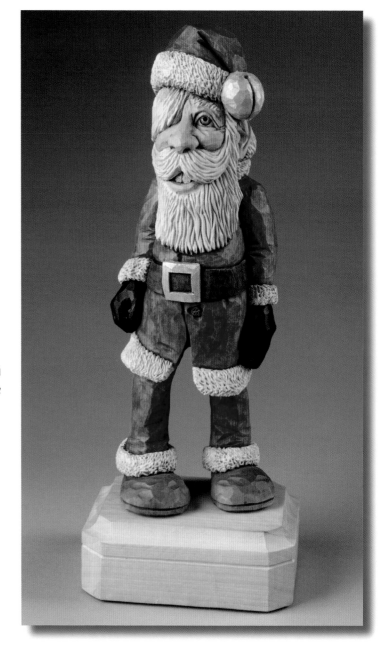

**Norseman**
*by Steve Brown*

**Santa**
*by Steve Brown*

**Battle Ready**
*by Mitch Cartledge*

**Jed**
*by Dale Green*

# Members' Gallery

**Chief**
*by PJ Driscoll*

**Play Ball!**
*by PJ Driscoll*

**Ho-Ho-Ho Santa**
*by PJ Driscoll*

**Red Cloud**
*by PJ Driscoll*

**Willie**
*by PJ Driscoll*

**Retired Cowboy**
*by Bob Travis*

**Amy**
*by Jim Hiser*

**Cloudy**
*by Jim Hiser*

# Members' Gallery

**Blockhead
Carver**
*by Pete LeClair*

**Sporty**
*by Pete LeClair*

**Charlie**
*by Pete LeClair*

**Bad Mad Madge**
*by Tom Wolfe*

**Red Hat Peggy**
*by Tom Wolfe*

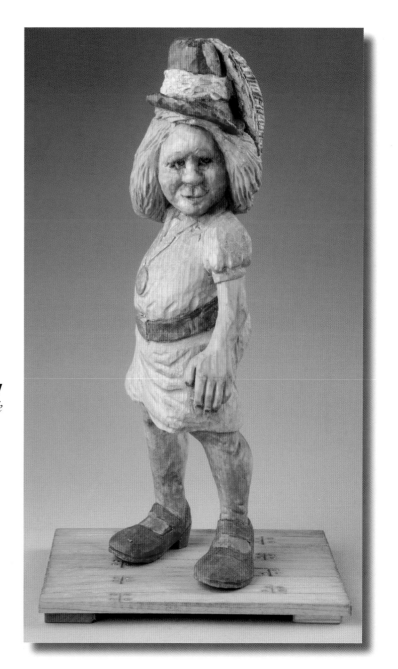

# Members' Gallery

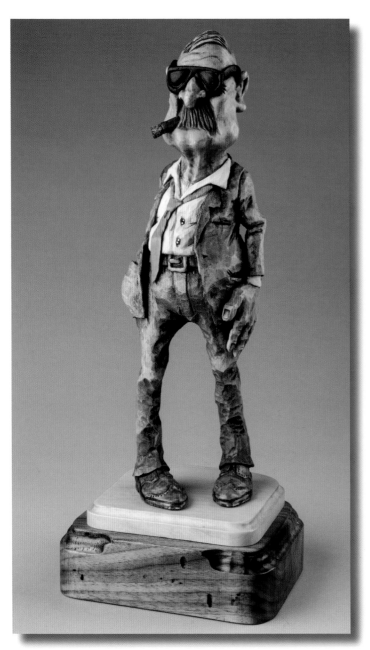

**Saul Goodman**
*by Phil Bishop,*
*Emeritus*

**Sancho Panza**
*by Pete Ortel,*
*Emeritus*

**Kitty
Kartrashian**
*by Vicki Bishop,
Emeritus*

**Mother
Nature**
*by Harold Enlow,
Emeritus*

**Caricature Carvers of America**

*Front row (pictured left to right): Chris Hammack, Ryan Olsen, Jim Hiser, Rich Wetherbee, Joe You, PJ Driscoll, and Gene Fuller (Emeritus).*

*Back row: David Boone, Bruce Henn, Joe Schumacher, Floyd Rhadigan, Dave Stetson, Dale Green, Dennis Thornton, Mitch Cartledge, Ron Dowdy, Wayne Laramore, Randy Landen, Sandy Smith, Bob Travis, Jack A Williams, and Steve Brown.*

*Not pictured: Gary Falin, Pete LeClair, and Tom Wolfe.*